What others are saying about this book

'Karen's experience in both work and life really shines through in her words. This book is a brilliant resource for anybody who is eager to understand the mechanisms behind their trauma, and also discover ways to help pull themselves out of the trenches.'

Claire Wakefield, Natural Body Lab

'This book is somehow personal and technical, skilled and relatable, technical and easy to understand – all in one. It's a memoir, it's a text and most of all it's essential reading whether you understand trauma is impacting your life or whether you just wonder why things are so hard all the time. Highly recommend.'

Natasha Berta, Connected Marketing

'This book is a must read for anyone dealing with trauma. It's a wonderful compilation of knowledge and wisdom gained through personal and professional experience by Karen. She brings a simple approach to many of the concepts where science and spirituality collide. This book is a testament to her dedication and commitment to her own healing and her service to others.'

Erin Miller – Intuitive Guide and Mentor

'Karen's quirky sense of humour combined with her innate amazing intelligence and insight make this a must read. Karen will take you on a journey to help you understand how dramatically our past traumas can and do impact us every day of our lives. While we think we are operating with what's presented in front of us, so often, that is not what is happening.

Most importantly, she focuses on looking for the gift or insights from each of these challenging situations that we've all been through so we emerge wiser and with more compassion for ourselves and others.'

Jacque Mooney, International Speaker, Instructor, and Author – Simply the Brain.

THIS IS MY ROAR

KAREN HUMPHRIES

This is my ROAR

Transform Your Trauma Tale

For my daughter Lulani, always my highest point of heaven, you are my inspiration to continue shinning my light. May I impart the skills you require to illuminate your own path forward. For my husband Andrew, thank you for quietly waiting.

For my brother Mark, for leading the way down the publishing path.

For the goddesses (Robi, Jen, Mettie) for the hugs,
laughter, shared tears and unconditional love.

For Tanya, for always saying 'yes I can'.

Contents

Introduction

How would you react if you opened your fridge door and a mountain lion roared in your face, swiping its claws at your eyes? Wait. What?

Your subconscious survival response likely kicks off with a gasp or shriek. If you're resilient, your grip on the fridge door handle tightens with the shock of the situation before you forcibly close the fridge door. Only then can you run for your life.

Right???

Would you even try to escape? Perhaps you might freeze on the spot? Would you become terrified of returning to the fridge again?

This book is about acknowledging that on some level and scale we all experience trauma in our lifetime. Navigating your trauma tale is challenging because you aren't born with resilience. This is a skill we develop through experiences by facing those challenges. **However, certain experiences are so significant that our resources for coping and responding are insufficient.** If this happens, some of us lack the ability to *respond* in that moment when we open the fridge to the mountain lion, and so we go into *reaction* or survival mode.

I adopted the phrase, *there's a mountain lion in my fridge*, from a post I read in a social media group for breast cancer patients. It felt so relevant to me. Everyone gets the metaphor when I describe how your stress response works in relation to the mountain lion.

A mountain lion can look and sound like a cancer diagnosis. It may look like the experience of a miscarriage. The death of a parent. Being made redundant at a job where the boss was bullying you and he got demoted but they still got rid of you. The sight of the mountain lion's teeth as it hisses can feel like a handsy parish priest at youth camp. Claw marks from that mountain lion can feel like a friend who took their own life. Scars from the mountain lion's scratch can feel like being in a car that rolls and crashes into a tree, leaving you bruised and concussed and your friend thrown out the windshield. The fear of opening the door to the fridge again can feel like a partner who yells at you because he is in pain with a spinal injury. A mountain lion jumping out of your fridge can even feel like being trapped in a mammogram biopsy machine.

I have a mountain lion in my fridge. This beast has matured and calmed as I have navigated my trauma tale. Through my personal and professional experiences, I now understand this creature. I recognise the mountain lion is wild and will never be tame, yet it is part of me. My response to the mountain lion in my fridge represents how I learnt to respond rather than react to life. I have learnt through these experiences about how to tame the mountain lion.

This book references trauma in terms of the event and provides information about how you react afterwards. You can't change what has happened in the past, but you can change your stress reaction to it. I call this reaction your trauma tale. This book presents examples of raw experiences, the science of how you subconsciously *react* in response to traumatic experiences, and how that reaction leaves you feeling raw. I share a collection of trauma tales with encounters of the mountain lion. I've included the tools I used to explore and use my roar in the hope you can heal your trauma tale too.

It's my hope that sharing these stories will reveal that you are not alone, nor the only one battling with your own mountain lion. You may wish to read the book from cover to cover, open at a resonating chapter or use it as a workbook.

This is a book for those who are seekers. You may have a trauma tale and feel stuck, and be seeking ways to dig your way out of the hole you feel you're trapped in. You may have a loved one who is experiencing symptoms of trauma and seeking information to understand their challenge. You may be a training practitioner and seeking the possible reason why your clients may feel stuck in their trauma tale.

I am a joy seeker, but to find the joy in my life I had to make sense of my trauma tale. As a *soul scientist* I combine my connection to a spirituality of sorts and mash it up with documented researched science.

THIS BOOK CAPTURES MY TRUTH, MY
NEW—FOUND RESILIENCE.

I HOPE THAT YOU TOO BECOME MOTIVATED TO
HEAL YOUR EXPOSED FEARS AND VULNERABLE PARTS,
JUST LIKE I DID. THIS IS MY REINVIGORATED
STRENGTH, MY PURPOSE AND MY PURSUIT OF JOY.
MY *RAW* IS A GIFT OF A COLLECTION OF EXPERIENCES
WHICH BECAME MY REASON FOR HEALING.

THIS IS MY STORY.

THIS IS MY ROAR!

How to become a mountain lion tamer

It's important to have an open mind when looking at where you're at in your life, especially your trauma tale, i.e. your mountain lion encounter. I've provided mountain lion taming instructions at the end of each chapter for you to learn how to pacify your mountain lion. Everything is designed to support the realignment of your thinking, feeling and how you do life.

Mountain lion taming includes setting intentions which relate to thoughts about plans to undertake specific action. Affirmations are positive statements that can support you to overcome negative, self-sabotaging thoughts. When you repeat affirmations often, and believe in them, you can start to make positive mindset changes. An *afformation* is where you utilise an affirmation as a question to identify how to implement your intention.

Affirmations are fabulous to create your intention at the beginning of the day. You can use them for goal setting. An alternative author of *The book of afformations*, Noah St John, identified the use of afformations that simply convert an affirmation to a question. Ask yourself, 'How would the intention for life via the affirmation be possible? What might life be like if you were living the embodiment of the affirmation or intention? How would you achieve it? The afformation allows you to explore how the heck you're going to get the good 'juju' back in your life! For example, the affirmation might be, 'I am safe in this moment', so the afformation would be, 'What would my life be like if I was safe in this moment?' It enables you to open that exploratory side of yourself without the fear running, and it allows you to stay in that calm place.

There are also *Suggested Journal Prompts* to support your own exploration of your trauma tale. These prompts are deliberately thought-provoking to coach you on how you can reflect on where you're at in your own life or trauma tale. Journalling is a powerful technique on so many levels as a subtle type of expression especially when you're caught up in your trauma tale. Journalling supports you when you can't find your words in the heat of the moment. The practice of writing allows you to defuse the thoughts that can continue to swirl around in your head long after your encounter with your mountain lion. If the journal prompts don't resonate with you, get creative with the intentions, affirmations and afformations.

When I prompt you to ask yourself some questions, answer them honestly. Allow yourself to get curious with the answers that arise. Don't shortchange yourself by responding with what you think is the right answer. Speak your truth to yourself.

We rarely reflect on how we're feeling or process our experiences. I call this *checking in with yourself*. It's a fabulous tool to bring yourself into the present moment and quantify where you are at, much like arriving at a guidepost and seeking direction. Our culture doesn't actively encourage you to self-monitor your ability to remain consciously present in your life. It's so easy to float along in life and migrate through the busyness of it or the entrapment of the mountain lion encounter. You don't realise that when you're stuck in the trauma tale, you're just surviving life – you're not actually living.

I want to gift you the opportunity or prompt you to reflect on your life as a movie. Consider any event that may have pushed your buttons and then ask yourself, 'Am I still in survival mode from that experience or have I been able to use it as the gift that it could be; one that's packed with opportunities to learn lessons, and therefore it could become a positive lesson-based outcome?'

Don't waste the opportunities that life gifts you. Live in the moment. When you recognise that you're not quite yourself or you've been feeling low for an extended period, even just two weeks, there's potential to develop subconscious reaction patterns called habits. Therefore, it's so important to connect with yourself.

Global exception

If after reading this book or completing the activities you continue to feel unlike your normal self, please act and don't remain trapped in the darkness within. I've been in the murkiness of wondering whether I will ever stand in the light again. Make that appointment with your preferred and trusted practitioner and start your return journey back to your vibrant, deserving and worthy self.

Additionally, a reasonable exception includes when sometimes a person's response to trauma may require medical intervention. I don't profess to be a psychologist, a psychiatrist or a Western medicine practitioner and I did not design the advice in this book to replace medical advice or support. If you've got a diagnosed condition, an ailment, a syndrome or a disease, I strongly advise you to manage that condition and symptoms through your diagnostic physician. If my suggested actions resonate with you, seek approval and guidance from your therapist for the best way to implement them under their supervision.

The various mountain lion taming activities suggested in this book have been designed as tools to support you in being proactive. Please note there may be times when you're feeling so stuck that you can't do anything proactive except survive. I'm simply sharing everything I find personally and professionally effective which I have gathered throughout the last 18 years that I've been doing facilitated change work and coaching. So, if you're feeling stuck within inaction, seek external support.

Chapter One

Recognise the roar

You can consciously transform your thinking and actions when you understand why your trauma causes an unconscious reaction.

This chapter discusses the importance of the human need for security. It explores the psychological definition of trauma and why you react. Your trauma tale is the accumulation of your reactions to stress from either a very significant event or exposure to long-term stress. It is your associated reactive stress response to the mountain lion.

Here, I'll explore why you need to develop a perception of a safe *tether*, when you're stuck in that trauma response of confronting the mountain lion in the fridge. Gaining knowledge of your trauma tale and why you perpetuate certain reactive behaviours opens the door to discovering ways to feel like you're tethered to a safe place. Only when you feel safe can you begin your healing journey.

Don't kid yourself, we all have stuff!

If you've followed me on social media or have seen me professionally, you will have heard me say to you, 'We all have stuff.' Life and our humanness are filled with messiness. All that stuff you shove under the carpet that you don't want to deal with! It's not going anywhere! Pretending it's not there or avoiding dealing with it simply drags you off the path of living and onto a busy highway where you must fight for survival. Is this any way to live?

Not dealing with your stuff also means you're adding to a pile of unfinished business, which can trigger your trauma tale. All those pesky, unknown or subconscious things that aggravate and frustrate you rise to the surface of your consciousness to consume your very breath. It's this unfinished business that drives your reactivity.

Many of the people I see in my clinical practice feel stuck within this reactive pattern of stress. By this I mean they have encountered a mountain lion in their life and haven't figured out how to shut the door on the fridge to feel safe. They feel trapped in their trauma responses (to the distressing experience) and it has become their normal everyday reaction to life: to survive rather than thrive.

Anthony Robbins is an acclaimed American author, coach and speaker. In his self-help book, *Awaken the giant within*, he introduces six human needs: certainty, variety, significance, growth, contribution and loving connection. The human need that stands out for me in terms of our trauma tale is the need for loving connection. The mountain lion challenges our loving connection to ourselves and others. When you are in a state of flight or fight, you are operating from a reactive mental state rather than the feeling centre of your heart. More on that later. In my clinical practice I support clients to defuse their stress so that they can heal their connection within themselves.

Discovering a mountain lion in your fridge can be so traumatic that it disconnects you, even momentarily, from your inner self and your own internal resources. This disconnection is a separation from the deepest and most sacred part of you. This interrupts your perception of feeling safe in your life and creates the trauma tale. It's this separation from this human need for loving connection that establishes the experience as reactive and stressful, leaving you unable to respond.

We all perceive the significance of the mountain lion encounter differently because we are all unique individuals. Any previous exposure to the beast can alter your subsequent patterns of reactive behaviour now and into the future. This adaptation of your neurological stress response to the mountain lion determines your resilience to respond or to continue reacting in the future. It's important to understand that this trauma response is where your resilient brain integration becomes dysfunctional, leaving you feeling dis-abled. This disconnection can happen to anyone. As Robbins explains, we all have this need to feel secure and safe in our lives now and in the future.

I have firsthand experience of discovering a mountain lion in my fridge. At the beginning of my breast cancer experience back in late 2019, I was trapped inside a mammogram biopsy-driver machine for over an hour.

This wasn't just a mammogram machine where your breast tissue is squished between two plates. This mountain lion was a machine that forces your breast tissue as flat as it can go. That machine caused me excruciating pain. Unfortunately, many local anesthetic applications were unsuccessful.

This machine uses a ramming biopsy needle driver to puncture through your skin to accurately obtain a biopsy sample where they suspect abnormal tissue, whilst undergoing live imaging. This machine also drives titanium tags to mark tissue for surgical extraction.

I was coping with the extreme discomfort until the ramming driver of the needle failed with the needle stuck in my breast. The computer wouldn't reboot, which left me stuck. I'm sure I passed out from the pain and the sheer shock of being entrapped within this machine, lying on my side with my arm over my head for over an hour. The entrapment was my reactive trigger that caused me to disconnect. My inability to act forced me to remain in a single position, held down, if you will, causing me to lose my tether to feeling safe.

I feel sick just thinking about it and continue to experience flashbacks of that afternoon. The mountain lion scored one that afternoon. I relate this entrapment experience to the human need for security that day. I lost my reference to feeling safe or having a safe tether in that situation.

Your beautiful brain

I believe the human brain is beautiful because of its complexity and ability to evolve. It allows you to be adaptive and creative, as well as socially connected. Your brain also provides an inbuilt subconscious survival program. Western science has identified that the human brain processes stressful situations through connections via our nervous system. When I studied brain integration with Jacque Mooney, I learnt there is constant transmission of information throughout your brain via your nerve cells.

All incoming information regarding the outside world travels up into your brain to a junction box called the thalamus. This is like a mail distribution centre that sorts out what to do with the incoming messages from the senses and the body in relation to what is occurring in the outside world. The thalamus sorts whether the incoming information requires more processing and forwards it to the executive function of the brain.

Your thalamus assesses your sensory data: what you see, feel, taste and touch, as well as motor information. Your thalamus determines where you are in your world. Near the memory box is your memory system called the hippocampus – not a hippopotamus – and the emotional processing centre of the limbic system (emotional processing centre).

Alongside the thalamus is the almighty amygdala, which provides an initial threat assessment and emotional colouring to all incoming and outgoing information. Your amygdala plays a role in your flight-fight-flee response.

Your amygdala assesses your perception of any situation. This perception is not necessarily real! You can perceive an experience as dangerous based on information being recalled from a previous event via information you recall from your memory systems. For example, imagine encountering a mountain lion in your fridge and struggling to escape. Do you think you'd be excited to return to the fridge and calmly open the door? Of course not! Your brain will extract the memory that there is a mountain lion in the fridge! The result is the brain will bypass the executive functioning and reasoning of the neo-cortex and seek a survival program instead.

Your thalamus and amygdala cross-reference information between short- and long-term memory in terms of whether you have experienced an encounter with the mountain lion before. The memory systems store a variety of information regarding whether you felt safe when you encountered the beast previously, as well as recording what actions you took in response to seeing the mountain lion. Your memory also records sensory data about what you saw, heard, touched, smelled or even tasted during an event. This means your amygdala rates each event with a level of significance that determines the depth of your response or reation.

Your brain rapidly attempts to find out what's happening in and around you in response to being frightened by encountering the mountain lion in the fridge. Your subconscious survival reaction is to fight, flee or freeze. During events in which you process loss of safety, the integration of your logic brain is challenged. By this I mean that your brain doesn't need to logically analyse data at that moment. Your brain bypasses the frontal cortex and runs a survival program to get you to safety.

In the moments it takes you to gasp in a breath of air after seeing a mountain lion in your fridge, your brain has signalled your heart to widen the vessels and transport blood to your large muscles to support you to get the heck out of that situation. The physical survival reaction is followed by the emotional program you've previously run when in survival, and this is when we have that Bridget Jones moment of 'holy crap!' Right at that moment the mountain lion scores a goal.

Modern humans' neurological threat assessment is identical to that which the cave dwellers experienced when encountering the sabre-toothed tiger. The neural messages from the amygdala, paired with retrieved memories, provide alerts to prime the sympathetic nervous system's flight-fight-freeze response, and your body with, 'We're not safe. You need to run or you need to hide.'

Peter Levine is a psychologist specialising in trauma and the author of *Waking the tiger: Healing trauma.* In his book, Levine reiterates the definition of trauma used by psychologists and psychiatrists as 'a stressful occurrence that is outside the range of usual human experience and causes distress'.

Levine discusses what would and could be reasonable to classify as 'outside the usual human experience' in terms of how the event triggered a person's primitive flight-fight-freeze response. Levine further explains that a trauma diagnosis should also link how the event subsequently made the person feel. I would add to Levine's description that a trauma-based response can interfere with a person's future ability to recuperate from encountering the mountain lion.

When you're in the traumatic event, everything feels like you're in slow-motion because your brain is gathering as much sensory data as possible to ascertain the level of threat, and comparing current data to that stored in your memory system. Therefore, you can so easily feel stuck, like you're frozen in time. It also explains why some people instantly want to run away or stand and fight. The response is subconsciously driven.

In that experience with the mammogram biopsy machine, I completely froze. I lost my power to speak up. I went into shock and I could not talk for about two or three hours after that incident. Because of that, I have experienced flashbacks and continue to be triggered by sounds like the drip machine and the smells of a hospital, which is challenging when, within eight days of diagnosis,

> I was having the first of six surgeries and twelve months of active oncology treatment.

Thanks to that mammogram experience, I have focused on my healing journey. The gift from that experience was to explore what it means to heal from encounters with the mountain lion. This reflective period highlighted that I have been working with trauma for about 15 years.

My reflections that the mountain lion was familiar surprised me. I've worked in emergency response with the Environment Protection Authority (EPA) Victoria and attended fatal accidents. I've been personally challenged, as well as supporting friends and family during times of crisis. These mountain lion experiences have all contributed to a strong, internal resilience library of responses. Working with war veterans, and sexual assault victims, has led to a good understanding and a working knowledge of how brain integration falls apart from the reaction to traumatic experiences.

Normal integrated brain function incorporates intact neural pathways whereby the whole brain is balanced and both left and right hemispheres are communicating effectively with each other. Dysfunction occurs in the brain when you activate your survival mechanisms and bypass communication throughout the entire brain, limiting neural pathways to activate a survival-based reaction.

Our brain is beautiful due to the myriad of functions it performs for us to keep us safe. Here's the thing: the brain doesn't know what is real or perceived at the subconscious level; it just records *thrive* versus *survive*. To recognise your roar, you must become consciously aware of your trauma tale.

From experience to trauma

I've already touched on how your brain's internal stress response works in very basic terms. Now we're going to make the connection between how your brain processes the information related to an event and how it classifies it as traumatic. When you understand how your brain works, you then understand how you react unconsciously and create patterns of that response.

The major neurological output pathway from the amygdala plays a role in anxiety. Mooney discusses that the pathways beyond the amygdala may mediate a slow-onset, long-lasting response to sustained threats. For example, when you need to return to the fridge but do not know whether the mountain lion is still inside, it can leave you feeling some trepidation. This means that the reaction to the threat can remain turned on long after the threat has passed.

Another part of the brain, the locus coeruleus, is associated with amygdala function and involved with your physiological response to stress and panic. It's the principal site for the synthesis of noradrenaline, which has an excitatory effect on most of the brain. This translates to heightening the flight-fight-freeze response including cognition, mood and blood pressure. When the locus coeruleus is activated, it creates a slow, mediated onset response to stress via the amygdala to enhance the loss of brain integration, i.e. logical thinking and function, and heightens your response to a perceived threat.

This is nerdy science stuff! I tell my clients that when the amygdala gets regularly involved, it's like you've invited a bunch of bikers to your house. They are drunk, high on acid and completely out of control! Your sympathetic nervous system activates the flight-fight-freeze response, which generates pathologies that look and feel like clinical depression, panic disorder, anxiety and even PTSD.

If you're still scratching your head and wondering how this all relates to your trauma tale, let me explain it like this. Imagine experiencing a mountain lion in your fridge and then not being able to turn off or diminish that frightened response. Now imagine that this reaction has become a habit and you perceive there is a mountain lion everywhere you go. Intense, right?

After the mammogram incident, my trauma tale was reactivated every time I had a surgery or oncology treatment, due to the sounds of equipment and smells of sterilised hospitals. I retrained my survival reaction with meditation and relaxation music to drown out the trigger sound.

I also used discreet amounts of aromatherapy in my hand moisturiser and hair conditioner, to reset my olfactory, sense of smell response to my environment. I was always mindful that those scents were subtle so as not to activate a sensory response within my neighbouring patients also undergoing treatment.

Smelling something pleasant whilst meditating was a very gentle way to reprogram my subconscious desire to run away from the situation. This is what makes our brain beautiful. Whilst our brains and neural networks are designed to keep us safe, we can retrain our reactions back to responses.

My approach in a clinical session

I am a kinesiology and wellbeing practitioner, inspiration coach and meditation facilitator. Predominantly, I work clinically with childhood sexual abuse and assault, domestic violence victims and people who experience *Post Traumatic Stress Disorder* (PTSD). At the time of publishing, I'm supporting many who are overcome by the fatigue of societal stress generated by the pandemic and extended lockdown.

In a previous role, working in the waste industry, I completed an investigations course that would be the equivalent of detective training. I am naturally inquisitive. I was inspired to pair my detective skills and kinesiology with my *mad scientist* methods to figure out the root cause of things rather than fluff about. Recovering from PTSD inspired me to become a truth seeker.

Kinesiology is a stress management modality, where practitioners use muscle monitoring to identify where the body may have an associated response or ability to maintain a reaction to stress. I'm observing how a client can remain present in a session: what their body language is doing, their ability to maintain eye contact, their ability to have open versus closed body language. I'm observing whether they are dissociated and checked-out or operating a survival program. I'm assessing their whole body and capacity in terms of physical, mental, emotional and energetic stress. In this instance, I am a detective in search of their roar.

Gathering data about someone's mountain lion encounter is also an integral component in a consultation. Knowing that your beautiful brain records sensory data together with the emotional flavour of all your encounters infers that the basis of your trauma tale can commence at a very young age.

When I work with clients, my questions are purposeful and designed to identify any potential trauma. My initial questioning attempts to capture evidence of positive experiences in your life as well. This creates a foundation of trust for hope and motivation. I work with my clients to unveil areas of life that could have the potential to be clinically perceived as a traumatic experience.

Life is full of experiences. Your birth, parental relationships and learning are just some basic examples of life events that can activate our survival program. Traumatic experiences can include events like car accidents, issues with friendships, workplace stress and learning challenges, through to sexual offences where the body has been violated. Even the global pandemic is a traumatic experience for many people within society.

Regardless of someone's trauma tale, my training has taught me to always seek consent to ensure the client always feels safe when they work with me. Remember Anthony Robbins's human need to be connected? Feeling safe is right up that survival alley. My whole job is to defuse any stress that has the potential to inhibit your ability to recuperate and be resilient enough to face your own mountain lion, should that ever happen. How can you possibly let down that defensive wall if you don't feel safe in my presence?

Robbins outlines the importance of being tethered and grounded. So, when I first see someone in a clinical perspective, I'm initially checking whether they're grounded in their body or whether they've disconnected. The reactive stress patterns can be so dramatic that they have subconsciously activated a flight-fight-flee reaction and not returned to their grounded state or sense of self. In some cases, clients have psychologically disassociated.

The American Psychiatric Association defines dissociation as *a disconnection between a person's thoughts, memories, feelings, actions or sense of who he or she is.* In this circumstance the person's stress reaction is so intense that recovery at the time of the initial event wasn't possible and the reaction has perpetuated into a subconscious habit of remaining in survival. A brief conversation will often highlight the significance of dissociation in terms of a person's ability to remain present in their own life.

Whilst conversation is very open, I empower the client by reassuring them we don't need to relive the mountain lion experience. The client is in charge of their session. It's my job to be gentle as I explore their reaction to the mountain lion, identifying where they lost their tether, that connection to themselves and back to that human need for safe connection and security.

Both my personal and clinical experiences have shown me that when I can support a person to feel safe, they're more likely to return to a state of calm and reconnect with themselves. This reconnection and perception of safety in the moment then activates the ability to feel secure enough to explore what's going on at a conscious level, instead of running a subconscious, fear-based reaction pattern.

The initial threat assessment run by the amygdala doesn't discern what is real and what's not; it just associates the sensory and motor input gathered and cross-referenced to earlier experiences in our lives, i.e. our memories. This means, if you have experienced the same data before, you repeat the same behavioural response. Therefore, you perpetuate the same response pattern. And if you're stuck in a trauma response, you need to feel safe enough to come out of it.

Clinically, what often causes the flight-fight-freeze response is our survival reaction or trauma tale. This stress-based reaction is often subliminal. You don't know the patterns that you run until you feel the symptoms of being stuck, such as anxiety, breathlessness or a tight chest. When you repeat that behaviour or response, it can leave you asking yourself, 'Where did this come from?'

When I work with clients on the conscious level and we unpack the source of the anxiety, the perception of feeling unsafe is often what brings us undone. Often, having a trained third party to guide your exploration of your trauma tale helps you to identify what fear is causing you to feel unsafe in that space of flight-fight-freeze.

I recall an incident when I was working with the EPA Victoria in my 20s. I was doing emergency response and it was my first solo gig, which was a fatal accident between a passenger car and a log truck. The incident report advised of fuel all over the road with the potential to pollute a nearby watercourse, as the passenger vehicle had ruptured the fuel tank of the prime mover.

Attending the site, I arrived before the Hazardous Materials (HAZMAT) Response Unit of the fire brigade, which meant that I had become the interim incident controller. I was greeted by a blood-spattered police officer who had wet patches on his pale blue shirt. I remember thinking how odd that looked and was mortified that I hadn't realised he had been crying. In my experience, that's quite unusual; normally police officers are stoic but now to see one crying put me on high alert. Something was seriously wrong.

I was about 300–400 metres away from the incident and I could hear wailing. I presumed someone must be trapped in the car.

The sergeant said, 'I know the victim in the car, she is my son's friend.'

My heart just dropped in that moment, and the dread settled in my gut. He was so distressed about how he would inform his family later that night. The wailing I heard was coming from the SES volunteers who had rushed to her aid only to discover it wouldn't be a rescue, but a body retrieval. They were all her friends.

As the incident controller, I had to stand down the response team and call in extra units. My training at the time didn't lend itself to providing grief or trauma support. In those eight minutes before the HAZMAT crew arrived, I remember I had to ignore the mountain lion pounding within me. I had to hold it together at the scene.

Looking back now, I realise I was on autopilot. I had shut down my emotional response to get the job done. It felt very much like an out-of-body experience. What I know now is that I had fled from my emotional response and that human need for safety.

What sits with me is the SES team's response to that incident. Not only had they lost their friend, but they were also trapped in that moment. Their flight-fight response had kicked in and they were all frozen in that moment, staring at their dead friend in the wrecked car. Most of them could not act or formulate words. They could barely walk. We had to physically walk them back to the safety of the ambulances waiting for them.

This is only one example of what a trauma response can look like: being stuck, untethered from your normal resilience resources inside yourself. Dissociation from your emotions in the moment allows you to move your body, but afterwards can leave you feeling very unsafe and insecure. This is what it means to be untethered.

For me, my response to the mountain lion that day didn't kick in until I was safe at home later that night when I cried myself to sleep. Twenty years after that incident, I still cry when I read the family's memorial notice in the local paper. The trauma of that day is reactivated by seeing what the female driver should have looked like, rather than the body I witnessed trapped in the car.

People often compare their experiences and their associated stress to those of others and then punish themselves with shame, blame and guilt when they perceive their own trauma isn't valid or real. During my breast cancer experience, so many people said to me, 'I shouldn't complain because what I have is nothing like what you're going through, Karen.'

I call it mind-reading. This is when someone has assumed or compared themselves to my thoughts and feelings and deemed them to be the same as theirs. Frankly, I call bullshit on that.

Never diminish what you feel from your experiences!

I pull them up straight away and say to them, 'Do you know what? We are given experiences to learn lessons. Who's to say that I didn't need quite a lot to learn my lessons? You've got no idea what I've been through in my life, so who are you to compare yourself to me? Only I walk in my shoes and wear my underpants! You are not me! I am me. You are uniquely you. So be you. How could you possibly compare your reaction to stress to what I have experienced in my life?'

You may experience the same level of trauma when your boss is having a bad day; perhaps this is all the time and they have spent the day raising their voice at you. This may have caused you to feel intimidated and frozen whilst being yelled at. Later you find yourself questioning what you did wrong and then overanalyse whether you're in trouble. Your feeling of dread about returning to the office could then be the same as when I was entrapped in that biopsy machine!

Stress is stress. We all have it in our lives. Life is messy. Your mountain lion encounter shouldn't be compared to someone else's because it doesn't serve either of you. What I suggest to people is to reflect on the following quote:

Make sure your worst enemy is not living between your two ears!

This means stop overthinking and overanalysing everything because it makes you bonkers. And don't worry, we're going to cover this later. In addition, consciously recognising that life is messy and we all have our own challenges gifts you permission to detach from the drama of others and just do you. This is how you learn to tame your mountain lion.

We've all been there

We've all experienced stuff in our lives that causes our knees to wobble. Being able to recognise the difference between survival stress and when your resilience is tested with a mountain lion encounter is interesting and useful for your healing. Survival stress is when you have a mountain lion in your fridge. You know, those moments when you open the fridge door and lean in unconsciously reaching for the milk only to have a mountain lion jump out at you? It strikes your arm and it draws blood.

What's the first thing you do?

People often answer, 'I shut the door again.'

There is an entire neural network supporting your brain's response called the sympathetic nervous system, which drives the subconscious *flight-fight-freeze* response. The amygdala sends a distress signal to the hypothalamus, which activates the sympathetic nervous system by sending signals through the autonomic nerves to the adrenal glands. These glands respond by pumping the hormone epinephrine, also known as adrenaline, into the bloodstream.

The first thing you do is suck in a huge breath. Your bloodstream is flooded with stress chemicals, which enlarge the vessels to send blood to the big movement muscles in preparation for actual flight or fight. Digestion and hormonal cycles are overridden. This flood of stress chemicals can make you feel sick in your stomach. It's only at this point several seconds later that your brain signals to your muscles to move your butt before the mountain lion takes a swipe at you.

The threat-assessment part of your brain tries to find where you've previously had a life-threatening experience and often that's when you learn to walk or do things for the first time. We all have subliminal memories of our parents yelling at us, 'Don't touch the hot kettle!'

As a child, you process your parents' frightened voices as, 'Oh, my God, this is life-threatening!' So, you've taken on the idea that the kettle must be scary. Then you have this whole pause-moment and your brain activates the freeze reaction for a second, until it kicks in again and signals to your hands, 'Move your muscles right now and take your hand off the kettle!'

Once you become familiar with the mountain lion and you've accepted it's in your fridge, it's time to feed it. You open the fridge and the beast roars at you while you throw a piece of meat at it and slam the door shut again. For me, this is what it felt like to experience PTSD or severe anxiety. You know the mountain lion is there. You recognise you're not yourself and you feel very stuck in that amygdala threat-assessment loop, also known as survival stress. It's challenging to dial down that survival stress response even after the perceived threat has ceased to exist, and it can be exhausting. In these moments you can't access your logical, integrated brain response because you are stuck in survival mode.

Working with a therapist enables you to feel safe after your mountain lion encounter and prepares you with strategies to reopen the fridge door using a tool that keeps you a safe distance away to observe the beast. It's only at this point that you realise the beast is chained up. Note, you didn't see that at first. The information you initially processed was a narrowed field of reality that included teeth and sharp claws but no chain.

During moments of PTSD response, you're not using any of your rational thought processes. You're in pure reaction mode. Your body's nervous system is programmed and wired like a caveman's, so your large muscles are primed to flee, fight or freeze. During these reaction moments, you completely sever your connection to reality and your perception of safety.

It's important to realise that in that moment of shock and the trauma response, no one is aligned to who they normally are. It's like you're floating. Remember, we all have stuff that causes our knees to wobble, but we need to recognise that there is a difference between moments of stress and experiences where your resilience simply doesn't hold up.

You might doubt that you've had a trauma experience. Perhaps this is because you compared your reaction to a stressor with someone else's reaction and you decided yours was not as significant as the other person's experience. We're all beautifully unique. We all have a different capacity to respond to stress and different resilience skills. Some need complex psychotherapy and others might just need to be reminded to do mindful breathing and nature walks to turn off the reaction.

 Mountain lion tamer tips

If your reactive pattern is outside your normal human experience, the first step to taming your trauma tale is to identify your safe place when you're feeling heightened. Make some time to create and maintain a routine that cares for your physical body whilst you do the healing work. Here are some basic tips:

1. Hydrate – drink at least two litres of filtered water each day.

2. Eat fruits and vegetables as they feed your brain the required nutrition to operate optimally.

3. Assess your sleep cycle:

   a. Go to bed at the same time every day and not too late.

> b. Don't eat two hours before bed.
>
> c. Switch off blue light devices two hours before bed.
>
> d. Limit consumption of sugars in the afternoon.
>
> 4. Make that appointment with a trained therapist.
>
> 5. Can't concentrate? Don't blob in front of the television, sit outside in the early morning sunshine whilst using lovely pencils to complete an adult colouring book.

People often need permission to just breathe when they are experiencing a trauma response. It's vital to remind yourself that you are likely to experience some resistance to change. This is common. The energy that you're consuming to run those fear patterns that continue to arise is enormous. When you're in survival mode you have limited capacity because of the threat reaction by the amygdala and energy needed while you're juggling all the balls of the stress response pattern. This means that your ability to seek a solution or different option or even move in a different direction is extremely limited whilst you are in a heightened state.

I'm not going to lie – initially when you face the mountain lion in the fridge, it can be uncomfortable, not to mention exhausting; however, not facing what is in the fridge means it has power over you, your responses and your happiness. The more often you confront your trauma response in a conscious way, the more you can deflate the threat the mountain lion has over you. It feels like letting air out of a balloon when you defuse the negative energy from your trauma tale. The energy of maintaining the negative reaction pattern dissipates and this allows you to realise that the mountain lion is tethered and can be contained, thereby allowing you to feel safe once gain.

When the past comes back to haunt you

Clients often ask me, 'Do you ever fix trauma?' I explain to people that you can't go back into your past and alter the actual event but you can diffuse the stress caused by how you've perceived the event. You can also break down the subsequent responses to a traumatic experience.

Being triggered by your trauma response links you back to that original amygdala activation of the initial threat assessment. The threat-assessment trigger turns on your sensory and motor inputs via your memory patterns and 'BAM' – the reactive behaviour activates! In my world, they call this neurological *survival switching*.

There are three survival switches that generate reactive responses, which result in you reliving any unfinished business from your encounter with the mountain lion. The three survival switches are:

- *Left to right* – distinguishing between the two spheres of the brain and attuning your logical and emotional response.

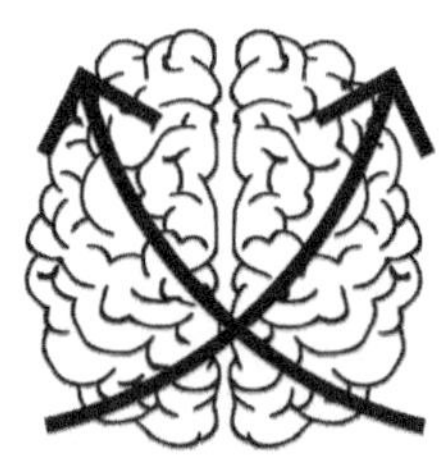

- *Top to bottom* – your amygdala fires inappropriately and you stop accessing the executive functioning of the neocortex and executive or higher-order brain functions, which include sensory perception, cognition, generation of motor commands, spatial reasoning and language.

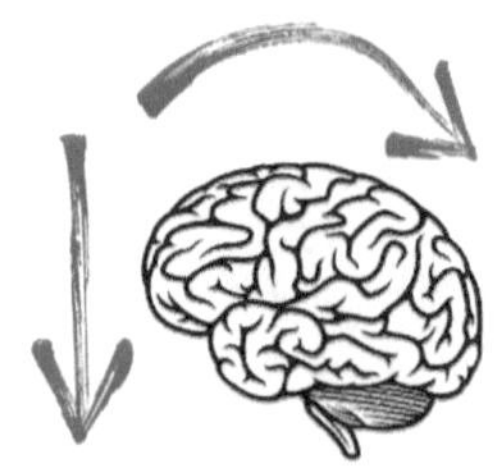

- *Front to back* – your frontal lobes contain all your solution-orientation and the primeval rear of the brain contains the most basic survival programs.

Activating a survival switch is when the dread sets in and the pattern of fear arises.

It's vital to understand how your trauma response can bite and leave scars. In society, there is a common desire that everything should have a quick fix or you require an external helper to help fix you (such as a therapist), or a magic pill or quick-fix potion. That just doesn't exist. You're responsible for and accountable to yourself for the quality of life that you live, and not just to exist.

I love working with kids who experience learning challenges. Unravelling their trauma responses can often occur in front of your eyes because they haven't formulated habits on their stress response yet.

I first saw Sarah before she started school. She was experiencing extreme anxiety and nightmares. In her young life she had experienced a lot of change; she had witnessed domestic violence and feared feeling insecure and abandoned. Subsequently, she displayed symptoms of anxiety every time her mother left the room.

Her front-to-back survival stress pattern was depicted as hysterical, inconsolable crying that only stopped when she ran out of energy to maintain it, which took several hours, every time. Sarah's top-to-bottom survival stress pattern depicted as an inability to form rational thought when her fear of abandonment was triggered. Her mother reported Sarah remained heightened for hours at a time, especially at night.

As soon as Sarah's survival switch was defused, she could picture feeling safe at night, safe on her own in a room alone and felt confident starting school.

Not every child I see in the clinic has witnessed what Sarah had. Sometimes a child feels and reacts the same way as Sarah when a sibling arrives in their world. Sometimes going to childcare or starting school is the trigger. Children are incredible energy receptors and will often react when an adult is intruding on their space, giving them the willies and a gut response that screams, 'Do not trust this person.'

Sometimes a child feels obliged to love the person who is harming them, such as a parent. They experience significant internal conflict when they both love and hate the person who is affectionate one minute and beating them the next, sometimes with words, other times with fists. Sometimes that child doesn't find their voice until they become an adult and finally encounters someone like me to whom they can tell their nasty secrets. If I had a dollar for every time I heard an adult say to me, 'I have told no one that this trauma happened to me,' I would be a millionaire by now.

When my clients are in the moment of realisation on a conscious level about what's going on with the pattern that they're running, I reassure them it can be incredibly confronting to recognise that they are stuck in that trauma tale. It's hard to step out of it. I'm not going to lie, it can take a ton of work. People ask me why that is and I tell them that it's because we've got the muscle memory of eating a 'shitty sandwich'. The wound that you have from that trauma experience needs to be unpacked bit by bit to learn the lessons of life. If you've been stuck in that reactive pattern, then you've developed habits that have infiltrated many parts of your life.

Your resilience is formulated initially through a combination of genetics and your environmental experiences. Your experiences dictate what's important to you in life and where you set your boundaries. Your values and beliefs influence how well you learn and develop your resilience firstly as a child, then as a teen, through to how competent you are with resilience as an adult. Many experts believe that if you experience trauma as a child between the age of two and seven, it can have a long-lasting impact on how well you live life.

# Mountain lion tamer affirmations to recognise your roar

Here's some suggested quotes and mantras for you to try:

Our beautiful brain

1. I no longer make my decisions based on the influences of my past.

2. In this moment I am safe.

3. I am worthy of peace.

From experience to trauma

4. I now allow my mind to be free of trauma.

5. In this moment, I allow myself to be free from the constraints of the past.

6. I now release suffering from my subconscious.

We've all been there

7. In this moment I choose to feel free and alive.

8. I release childhood memories that are causing me trauma now.

9. It's good to be me.

When the past comes back to haunt you

10. I release the need to be controlled.

11. I can heal in my own time frame.

12. I grant permission to detach from my past and anchor into today.

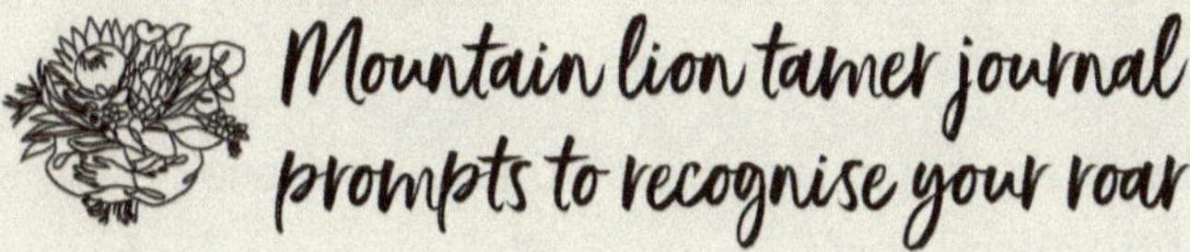 **Mountain lion tamer journal prompts to recognise your roar**

Our beautiful brain

1. When I am triggered, I find myself more defensive or proactive because...

2. How well do I cope when things get tough?

3. Do I feel stuck or can I easily move forward with life?

From experience to trauma

4. Where is my safe place and why?

5. If I'm honest, where or with whom do I not feel safe? Why?

6. If I were willing to explore, what would I discover about what drives my anxiety or sense of not feeling safe?

We've all been there

7. What scenarios trigger me to sometimes feel alone in my thoughts and feelings about life?

8. What is the consequence of these thoughts and feelings?

When the past comes back to haunt you

9. Have I ever experienced an encounter with a person, place or event that stresses me out? Why?

10. What positive thing could happen if I could hit the pause button and feel safe to explore the trigger?

11. Where in my life do I diminish or downplay my negative experiences? What do I gain from this?

12. What might it feel like if I could finally release how the past treats me now?

Chapter Two

Flick the switch

It's challenging to be strong and ready to run at the same time — it's one or the other.

This chapter discusses how your brain works and what happens when you activate your survival switch. There are different levels of switching. The first is situational and it's triggered by experiences such as lack of sleep or having a bad day. Depending on the severity of the trauma, you can utilise your resilience resources to step out of this momentary survival reaction.

The second type of neurological switch involves a deep survival reaction, which triggers a negative, reactive behavioural pattern. For some people, a deep survival switch means they are living this survival pattern 24–7.

Let's explore the different survival switches; these are front to back, top to bottom, and side to side. Understanding the effect of survival switching in your brain, you can appreciate the effect of loss of integration, which generates reactivity like flight, fight or freeze.

Source - Canva, 'Colour Vector'

Survival switching is a form of reactive, neurological defence. Picture your nervous system holding up fists ready to fight! Switching keeps you safe in situations where you're under threat, but you don't realise that you can keep this survival mechanism turned on unconsciously.

This reactive state can cause mental confusion and issues with defence in your body. It can create compensation patterns and it can reduce your ability to remain flexible and open-minded. Deep-seated, reactive behaviour directs your ability to impact or remain present in the 'here-and-now' and to cope with life rather than feeling like you're afraid of it.

In his book 'Waking the Tiger, Peter Levine discusses the *orientating response*. This is where your field of vision incorporates what you see and focuses on what's directly in front of you. It also incorporates how the brain gathers data on what you think you see when detecting movement or sound within your peripheral visual field.

When movement or sound activate your peripheral visual and auditory fields, your brain processes this sensory information with two key threat assessments. Where is it coming from? Is it a threat? Your natural response is to become either curious or go on alert. This unconscious threat assessment creates a kinesthetic awareness that links into a harmony between your ability to use your body and to express yourself.

However, if you have an unresolved trauma response, your resources for this orientation-reflex become reduced. As soon as the threat assessment begins, your old unresolved reaction to trauma is recalled from your memory. Your brain runs a reactive behavioural survival program, even though the threat is likely to no longer be present. Your brain activates an unconscious neurological response, which drives your flight-fight-freeze response. The more you activate this, the more you add emotions to your survival program and repeat the sequence over and over again. This is how your stress response habit forms.

In this chapter, I will discuss how these defence mechanisms work and how you can turn survival mode off, to roar again. I'll also discuss how you get to return to taking action rather than being stuck in reaction.

Turn the lights back on

What happens when you're doing survival switching? What can it feel like? Her teacher encouraged the nun and Buddhist monk Pema Chodron to inspect the knee-jerk reaction when you have a mountain lion in your fridge. Chodron talks about how you move away from the present moment when things get uncomfortable or challenging to face. Chodron refers to this as *shenpa*, which translates as 'attachment' or 'hook into the uncomfortable'.

Chodron explores how in our Western society we strengthen this habit of escape as young children. We learn to choose fantasy over reality. We get comfortable in leaving our thoughts and worries. What I've come to learn is you do this because you are paralysed in the trauma response of survival. You get lost in your thoughts. You disconnect from reality to give yourself a false perception of security – back to that human need.

Chodron explored these hooks of when you feel stuck. She likened the hook to having an itch and wanting to scratch to make the itch go away. She recognised that while scratching the itch makes the itch go away, it doesn't deal with why the itch has appeared. The itch is simply the conscious awareness of being triggered by something and that itch gives you the opportunity to get curious. Scratching is the itch repeating the hook on your stress trigger pattern. When left unchecked, your shenpa or hook is like a highly contagious disease and spreads to many aspects of your life until everything makes you itch.

When you break that down and look at your neurological deep survival switching, the itch can look and feel like frustration that escalates into anger or rage. This is where you're suppressing or overly expressing your thoughts and feelings. Your hook is triggered by current events but often it links back to different times in your life when something traumatic occurred and you haven't recovered from that experience yet. Therefore, when you are hooked, when you have activated your shenpa, you are not present in this moment; you are simply reacting to something from your past or projecting your fear of something into the future.

This hook can make the itch so uncomfortable that your amygdala turns on a strong defence response and you run the reaction pattern of escape, submit or freeze. This is where the itch is so uncomfortable that you need to escape. It feels like you want to run or leave a relationship without resolving what it's all about; you just need to get out of there.

Internally, it can feel like a need to retreat and escape to a bedroom or watch TV, or in the worst-case scenario, you split off or dissociate and you daydream or fantasise. The survival-switch reaction can sometimes feel like when you can't stand up for yourself and you become that deer in the headlights: paralysed in that moment and unable to act. Alternatively, this survival reaction can also feel like the need to be passive and not rock the boat to feel safe – that human need again.

You can also experience pain, punishment, panic, sadness, grief or depression when switching. With this type of deep survival switching, you can have a fear of something, for example, fear of punishment, failure or not being good enough. This fear is often far worse than the real thing eventuating. It's often associated with perpetuating a program linked to self-punishment, shame and blame or guilt.

When you have switched to survival mode, you run various emotional responses like fear, threat, danger, pain or punishment. The fear usually creates a false misperception that can be worse than reality and leads to controlling behaviours and habits such as the need to control.

The final psychology component of deep survival switching links with what you block when you experience the negativity previously described, your pleasure or reward programs. This is all the negative feelings from the survival stress contributing to blocking your ability to experience pleasure or the reward of life. When this component of survival switching activates, it blocks the internal perception of life being enjoyable. When your perception of the reward of life becomes blocked by survival behaviour, you can perceive joy of life is not deserved. This leads you to become overly critical of yourself and to feel unworthy and not good enough. When you don't feel like your best self, you dim the light that you shine to the world. It's powerful stuff, isn't it?

Chodron explains that since childhood you have strengthened your habit of escape and chosen fantasy over reality. You get comfortable in leaving your stress rather than dealing with it. You lose yourself in your thoughts, your worries and plans for the future. This avoidance creates a false sense of reality, just like scratching the itch and making it go away. But unfortunately, the more you scratch, the more heightened your brain's response to potential threats becomes. You can't move forward in your life. Your switch gets activated subconsciously and you can't turn it off. You subsequently assess everything as an actual threat. There is where the perception of fear becomes activated.

When you've got a survival switch occurring, you can't thrive or grow in this mode; you're only existing.

An example of this is Jenaya. She came to my clinic with a lack of joy in life. She was highly emotional and crying all the time. Her sleep cycle was fractured. The hormonal cycle was all over the shop. I identified she had a deep survival switch linked with stress on her heart-self points: her ability to love herself and experience joy without judgement. When we explored all the associated symptoms of deep survival switching, she explained, 'I'm all in my head and I'm misperceiving everything.'

The more we unpacked the layers swirling around her head, the more I could show Jenaya she was running a compensation pattern to being disconnected away from her heart space, that place where she should be grounded and should link with positive emotions and energy systems. This compensation presented as avoidance and distraction and completely consumed her life, making her want to become too busy all the time.

She believed she needed to be in control because she felt anxiety. This compensatory defensive pattern was deeply ingrained, causing her to not be able to let go of her triggers or face her shenpa; she was constantly scratching her itch. The flow-on effect of not letting go and overanalysing everything meant Jenaya had no ability to trust herself and her decisions or instinct. The survival stress pattern of avoidance left her feeling constantly unsafe. To combat this raw feeling, she attempted to control everything.

Does this sound familiar to anyone? Remember, everyone has these subtle hooks that drive unconscious habits! So, you often run these behavioural programs without a second thought until you feel yourself falling into a dark, bottomless pit without the energy to get out again.

You only exist in one location: your heart or your head. The fundamental basis is that you're either in your heart connected to your innate wisdom and grounded within yourself, or you are in your head. Ideally, you should resonate between the two in harmony to ensure you aren't stuck in your feelings or analysis.

If your amygdala is doing the unhappy dance and causing you to react to everything with the deep survival switch activated and living in your head, you can even split off from your centre of being. Here the amygdala runs you, rather than being heart-brain balanced, which is the place where you experience joy and happiness and love. If you're in your head, you've disconnected because you're running a survival switching stress pattern and you're stuck in the rawness of life experience.

'Doesn't everybody feel like this?' is the question I'm frequently asked by clients. My response is always, 'Absolutely yes!' We all have experiences in our lives that teach us lessons and push our buttons. However, the exclusion is you don't want to remain in a raw state. You want to live a life where you are connected into your heart and your light shines brightly.

Everyone experiences neurological switching and you do experience self-doubt at some points in time. We all experience traumatic events in our life. Some are significant, others we readily overcome.

For example, you can get a fright from a police car driving behind you with the lights flashing and you have that moment of panic, worried that you're about to get booked for speeding. Then the police car passes you and heads off. Your amygdala recognises the threat is over, your memory systems take over, you take a deep breath and you're fine. Within an hour, the cortisol which has surged into your body to respond to a threat dies down and you're back to normal.

If you've had a negative experience earlier in your life with a police car or emergency services flashing lights and that triggers your deep survival response, you can become triggered in the police car scenario above. Depending on the severity of your previous trauma, you can become stuck in that trauma response and all day, or week, or worse, for the next month, you're heightened. Our ability and our resilience to respond to that mountain lion (that may or may not be in the fridge) links with how strong that survival stress response habit is. It is the strength of the switch that determines whether you can *roar*, or if it leaves you feeling *raw*.

If you've got a deep survival switching pattern activated, you might feel you don't know what's wrong with you. You feel heightened for no apparent reason. You might feel stuck or potentially overwhelmed, or you can't actively shift yourself out of that state of feeling stuck and it causes you to feel panicked. Your survival switch may leave you unable to concentrate or lacking clarity at the moment. You may experience fears or anxiety.

This is a great stepping-stone to discuss survival switching and what's happening inside your head. We'll talk about breathwork in the next chapter and how you can get grounded outside. For now, pause and drink some water and be sure to remain hydrated.

Mountain lion tamer tip to turn your lights back on

Hold your *Emotional Stress Release (ESR) points at the* front of the forehead and back of the head. The frontal cortex of your brain contains all the present moment resources and identifies solutions. When you aren't switching, your brain operates executive functions to resolve the challenge in present time with a balance between our logic and emotions. 

The back of the brain contains association resources that are linked with long-term memory. Holding your hand at the front and back of your head promotes the flow of oxygenated nutrient rich blood to your brain. It also signals your frontal cortex that there isn't a mountain lion in front of you and to go find a solution to calm down.

Reboot your computer

There are three types of survival switching: front to back, top to bottom, and side to side. Let's explore how you can lose brain integration, how to keep your ability to respond and your roar response, rather than returning to a squeak and a panic in that survival program.

Top to bottom switching is where you can integrate positive emotional responses to your experiences, leaving you feeling *raw and reactive.*

Craig first came to see me to address his anger outbursts. He was negatively fixated on everything in his life. He found life itself challenging and had difficulty returning to a calm state and rational thinking when he felt triggered. He said, 'Everything is setting me off.' He felt it was impossible to reflect and learn from the trigger and he was overthinking everything, experiencing that merry-go-round of the same raw emotion, stuck in the flight-fight-freeze program.

He had activated the fear of judgement and self-punishment. When we explored what was going on, he agreed he was in a reactive mode. His brain wasn't accessing the higher executive function of the neocortex, therefore there was very little problem-solving occurring. He reported feeling stuck and very raw. To exacerbate his fears, he felt terrible guilt for being a bastard towards his family and friends.

In the first part of this chapter regarding top to bottom switching, I explained how information comes into a junction box called the thalamus which processes all that sensory information as well as what the motor coordination is doing. Then it sends that information to different parts of the brain. Top to bottom is where you access your higher-order thinking to reason and then respond calmly with solution-orientated thinking. If you're not doing top to bottom processing, you're just reacting and not responding.

Side to side switching involves the two spheres of your brain: one that processes logical thinking and one that processes emotional and creative thinking. Some people have this type of switching where they can't tell their left from their right.

> I have a friend Magda, who is a little scary when driving. The map will direct us where to go. She will point with her left hand but say 'turn right'. Magda always laughs, 'Oops I did it again'; meanwhile I'm left crapping myself in the passenger seat. She has this laterality confusion where she cannot tell left from right. She has to point where she wants to go because even her words are confused when it comes to her sense of direction.

This confusion may interfere with your learning. When you're in a classroom, for example, this can mean that you're missing learning opportunities because your brain isn't switching on the correct learning part, and therefore children can become emotionally heightened in a classroom because their brain is switching all over the place. These children's brains cannot sort out the mental information to learn and then embed it in their memory. This is because the information is being sent to the incorrect part of the brain to initiate processing; this takes more time and energy, if it is to be done at all.

When I'm in clinic and defusing a deep survival switch, I explain to the client that their reactive response is simply to visit their archive room out the back, because they're using a survival program to get them through this moment.

> The day that I received my surgical pathology results, what we thought was my cancer diagnosis ended up being much more serious. The moment that my doctor told me, I had that panic of being trapped back in that machine and unable to run away.

I wanted to escape this new reality that I would now require oncology treatment to reduce the chance of developing metastatic return within two years. That feeling that my daughter might not reach adulthood with her mother was just horrifying for me to process.

I remember not being able to think logically or find a solution at that moment. It was like I was opening the door to the mountain lion all over again. I cried because I'd activated all this fear: fear of death, fear of my child losing her mother and this grief of losing the expectation of how I thought my life would unfold. In those moments after the doctor left, I held my Emotional Stress Release Points (ESR points) and just allowed myself to grieve the expectation of how life might have been.

Most people don't realise that you have this inbuilt protection mechanism of deep survival switching. This switch is very much your unconscious caveman response and designed to keep you safe from a saber-toothed tiger. It's not until you attempt to live your life that you realise you're stuck in the raw reactive pattern.

For example, imagine a child who has a learning challenge. Their parent or teacher can't support the heightened child until they see the behaviours being activated. If the child's survival behaviour is to freeze or flee, then a parent could readily judge the child to be lazy or faking anxiety symptoms. Lack of brain integration in a child isn't just behavioural. They might have poor writing, delayed speech, can't read properly, their handwriting looks like the Richter scale or their learning milestones are slow.

You don't often recognise that your internal dialogue relating to shame, blame or guilt is part of a self-sabotage pattern that comes from when you've activated your survival switch and can't turn it off. Your sense of self-worth diminishes when there is a stress on your learning capabilities, especially if you are slower than those around you. When stress builds up, you can be very harsh with yourself and your internal dialogue. You become your own worst critic but you don't make the correlation that you've simply activated your raw, reactive survival switch.

ALWAYS REMEMBER, YOU ARE A PRECIOUS CHILD OF THE UNIVERSE, DESERVING OF FEELING SAFE, WORTHY AND OF BEING LOVED.

I often prescribe homework for clients to reinforce the work we do in the clinic or workshops. When you work on healing your trauma tale you will slowly realise when you have turned on your survival switch because you will recognise that raw and reactive feeling. You can use points within your energy system called meridians discussed in chapter four in 'Meridians – get flowing'.

 **Mountain lion tamer tip to reboot your computer**

1. Rub switching points when feeling fluffy, i.e. loss of clarity.

2. Switch On is great for when you feel triggered or stressed.

   a. Rub each of the three points with neutral touch (opposite) + navel.

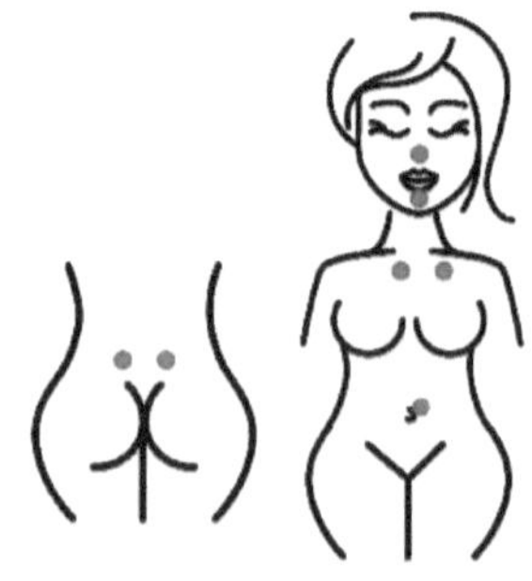

   b. Above and below both lips (end points of central and governing meridians), make a 'u' with your hands and rub.

    c.   Below the start of each collarbone off the sternum (end points of kidney meridian).

    d.   End of tailbone.

    e.   Now swap hands as these neutralise the polarity or energetic charge.

    f.   Note the navel is a master meridian point.

3. Zip Up.

    a.   Run your fingers stuck together from your pelvis to just under your bottom lip (the central vessel meridian).

    b.   Repeat three times.

    c.   This reinforces the natural flow in this central meridian and can unlock any energetic imbalances, especially for energy which needs to leave the body.

We all have built-in survival switches that keep us safe from the mountain lion in the fridge. There's no quick fix. Sometimes, when you're working on deep survival switching patterns, it feels like you're winding back the dial slowly and your shenpa makes you feel very uncomfortable in that space. At other times, you can turn the switches off and revive integrated brain function.

In a trauma response, it's hard to recognise that your adaptive behavioural patterns, like anxiety, are from when the switch was first created. In your trauma response you're just dealing with the pattern in the present moment. Healing can only begin when you realise your reaction is no longer serving you. You need to say to yourself, 'This doesn't work for me anymore; now I'm really ready to change.'

When you get thrown a curveball

When I discuss *brain integration* I am referring to entire neural pathways remaining fully operational and used to live a full life. During times of stress your neural signals can be rerouted, areas bypassed to pathways of least resistance, in order to rapidly activate your survival program. What this means is you don't need to analyse why there is a mountain lion in your fridge. Your brain's survival mechanism simply activates a process of survival at any cost.

Let's link what's happening within your brain in relation to your ability to maintain integration rather than survival. Let's discuss psychological conflict and reversal, and how you perceive those emotions that I spoke about before: the anger, rage, frustration, all the way through to the raw, reactive state of blocked pleasure and reward. When your survival switch activates, you can easily misperceive the world around you. This misperception impacts your ability to believe in yourself and to think that you're capable of change, let alone feel safe in it. You then create a *stress-avoidance* cycle. This is when you've been scratching the itch, your shenpa, and avoiding all things uncomfortable.

If you're stressed about something, you lose a portion of brain integration. It's like your amygdala is doing an unhappy dance and your nervous system is reacting to that feeling of a biker gang inside your body having a rave party. When you lose brain integration by flicking the survival switch on, the result is that you can become frustrated with yourself. You lose your ability to think clearly and feel calm in that moment. From an external perspective, people can misinterpret this behaviour as being directed at them. This is because shenpa is activated and you are in your own raw, reactive state. We truly are complex critters.

WHEN YOU BECOME STUCK WITH YOUR SURVIVAL SWITCH ON, YOU OVERREACT. YOU CREATE IMAGINED CONSEQUENCES RESULTING IN A PERCEPTION OF PUNISHMENT.

Picture this. Your shenpa itch is twitching with someone reacting to you or responding to you in the present moment, then potentially you misinterpret their body language as a negative response. The reason for this is your brain has retrieved information from your memory system about the previous traumatic event and something in this current encounter looks, smells or feels like that previous encounter, task, place or person. Your amygdala goes bananas with the threat assessment and triggers a chain reaction in your body that basically puts you on high alert. This is where all the stuff went down!

The survival switch gets activated because your memory systems have retrieved your previous reaction to the original event, so you don't have to create a new program in this moment, you just have to survive. Now you repeat your response to the original trauma event. This is where your brain is reinforcing your initial raw reaction from the initial negative experience. And so, the trauma tale habit begins.

Your raw reaction can even be triggered by other people's responses – verbal and non-verbal – to you feeling stressed out! This is how your survival stress builds and erodes your resilience. This leads to the creation of the foundation of fear of failure. From that heightened sensation caused by the survival switch being turned on, you then want to avoid feeling fear. You avoid fear because that sensation takes you away from the human need for feeling safe.

To compensate for feeling heightened, you create behaviours to avoid fear of failure. You spiral down to what is the most simplistic, basic thing you need to do in this moment to survive. The consequence of this is an erosion of brain integration and use of your higher order thinking that supports your self-worth, your self-belief and your confidence. It just flows on and on and on and the pesky mountain lion scores another point.

Complex right? And yet, when loss of brain integration was explained to me like this, I experienced a massive 'Aha' moment regarding my trauma tale. Suddenly my overprotective and defensive behaviours made so much sense.

When you lose brain integration and are running a trauma tale, it can feel like you must claw your way back to feeling safe and normal. This is a natural defensive response that you've learnt from the mountain lion: defend yourself before someone can hurt you first! You do this to protect yourself from feeling like crap or experiencing even more fear.

You actively run survival programs to avoid feeling helpless and you naturally digress to actively seeking the need for control. In those survival moments you misperceive that if you can control just one thing, you can feel good about yourself. In those controlling moments you fail to see that you aren't actually living your life, you are merely surviving it and missing out on opportunities to thrive. Whilst operating deep survival switching, you maintain Chodron's hook of what triggers your reaction.

An example of this is a young woman who experienced debilitating anxiety. Tracey's survival switch was activated by interactions with her workplace colleagues. Tracey worked in a call centre where her performance was statistically micromanaged and assessed on every single customer call. With each call, she only had a few minutes to perform in a certain way with customers, regardless of how they behaved. She quickly became defensive and reacted to a personality difference with her supervisor, which caused conflict.

It didn't take long for Tracey to develop a fear of being observed, and she rapidly declined with the new belief that she wasn't good enough. Working with her, we discovered that 'fear of failure' then triggered her debilitating symptoms of anxiety and depression.

Every time she sat in front of the computer and put a headset on, her shenpa itch began. Imagine now Tracey's amygdala threat assessment reporting to her thalamus, 'This is no good, we're not safe here.' Tracey had a false perception that she wasn't physically safe doing her job. Her response was a military control of her behaviours to override this misperception. She had to control everything. She ate at a certain time, a certain amount with everything measured out. She needed to control counting, actioning and rechecking locked doors, because those were the things that she could control. When she couldn't consciously control things, her anxiety was through the roof.

This perception of not being safe rapidly escalated to behaviour, which included irrational thinking processes and escalated to a highly emotional state; she felt out of control. Tracey's frustration and anger were unmanageable and there was an altercation at work that resulted in disciplinary action. She couldn't understand why she, as a pleasant person, was constantly feeling overwhelmed and it left her completely frazzled.

Tracey lived with these symptoms for over two years, attempting a variety of natural therapies until her anxiety caused out-of-control panic and she was prescribed medication to reduce symptoms. The medication provided only temporary relief before the symptoms returned. We had several sessions very close together to address the root cause of her survival switching.

Nowadays, Tracey has implemented long-term changes to her self-care routine to manage her stress, which improves her ability to cope. For Tracey, going to work was as if she were opening the fridge door and having a mountain lion jump out of it every single time.

When I work with clients and identify a deep survival switch, they are only aware of the defensive nature of their behaviour without understanding the cause or trigger. This is because the survival program that your brain runs to survive is subconscious. Your brain doesn't make you consciously assess every process or program run in the body. Imagine having to think constantly 'breathe now, pump your heart now'. You don't realise you're unconsciously hooked until the symptoms make you uncomfortable and you begin to itch or you are so intense that it forces you to pause and realise that 'I'm stuck in this raw, reactive response.'

Often, it's not until you explore why you're switching that you realise your behaviour has declined into an overreaction and you've entered that cycle of shame, blame or guilt. It's not until you're doing the behaviour or feeling it building up discomfort in your body that you can acknowledge, 'I'm hooked on something here. I'm being triggered. If I can look at it, I can do something about it.' As uncomfortable as they are in some ways, those symptoms are a gift to you to uncover something subconscious.

Chodron talks about how the shenpa hook is a gift. Practise allowing yourself to check in when you're triggered by something and realise, 'I don't need to scratch the itch right now, I can allow myself to feel the itch and ask myself, "What's really going on? What's under this? What's this all about?"' Yes, you can crave the chocolate, a cigarette or a drink, but when you allow yourself to explore what the itch is, you learn a lot about yourself and you fast-track your healing.

> -💡- **Mountain lion tamer tip to catch the curveball**
>
> Go within. Spend a little time reflecting on what might trigger you. I've included some *Suggested Journal Prompts* to support you in gaining an understanding of where your buttons get pushed. Identifying those triggers, supports you in healing any old destructive patterns that no longer serve you because we all have them.

What did we learn?

I often say to people when we talk about switching, 'Congratulations, you've just covered the basics of neurobiology 101 when it comes to survival switching.' In my experience, my clients get that 'Aha' moment when they understand that the caveman response is normal for every living thing on the planet. It's more than just flight-fight-freeze in that moment when you're standing in front of a mountain lion. Human beings are amazing at adapting to the environment. Your survival switch is useful to keep you safe in moments of danger. But your challenge is being able to turn the switch off to feel safe again and not continue reacting.

It's valuable to gain an understanding of how your body responds in stressful moments and support yourself to consciously recognise when your reactive pattern has been activated. You are responsible and the person who must resolve it. When your awareness is conscious you can take proactive steps to your own healing.

There's a societal notion about seeking a magic pill or a quick fix. That doesn't exist. You've spent years developing these patterns and there's no one quick thing that will undo it or take it away from you.

What's coming up?

So far, I've talked about Western science and how the brain works, but there's another piece of our biology puzzle: how we use our breath to transform our trauma tale. That's coming up in the next chapter. From this point on all references to switching refer to the examples of the deep survival switching, which alters your behaviours.

Mountain lion tamer affirmations to flick your switch

Here are some suggested quotes, actions and journal prompts to explore:

Turn the lights back on

1. I am capable of change.

2. I accept this is who I am in this moment.

3. With every breath I take, I feel more and more relaxed.

Reboot the computer

4. I release all internal conflict and distress, and activate my inner peace.

5. I release my reaction now, so that I remain empowered.

6. I clearly see my triggers as lessons to be embraced.

When you get thrown a curveball

7. I let go of the need to please others.

8. I have the courage and confidence to pursue my dreams.

9. I always have choice and I choose me.

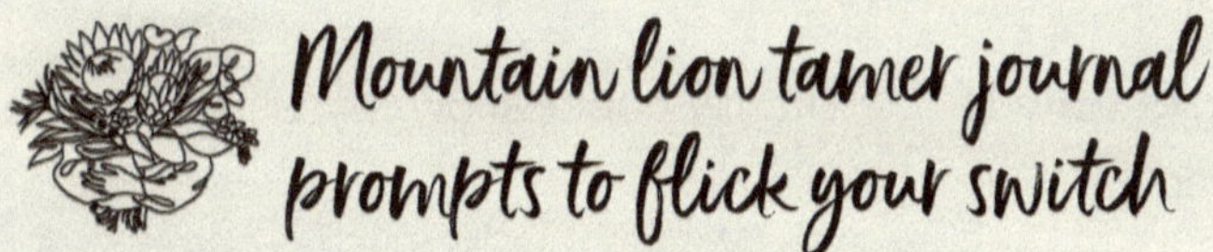

Mountain lion tamer journal prompts to flick your switch

The journal prompts you might like to ask yourself are:

Turn the lights back on

1. What are my survival emotions that I experience?

2. Is there a pattern of these emotions in my life?

    a. If yes, write a story about what this pattern might relate to.

    b. What types of situations will trigger these emotions or cause me to react?

    c. How well do I deal with these emotions? How do I react? Is this response constructive or destructive?

    d. How long does it take to relax after being triggered?

3. How might others see me or what might they think and feel about how I deal with my emotions?

4. If nothing above registers with me, do I see this in anyone else around me and is my stuff being reflected back at me?

Reboot the computer

5. Where or with whom do I find myself feeling reactive before I'm even in the room with this person? And why is that? What is the actual feeling arising here?

6. What event, place or person do I dread spending time with? Why? Allow yourself to get curious and write a story about the hook.

7. What might my life be like if I could allow myself to release the dread?

When you get thrown a curveball

8. Is there a place, person or time that causes me to itch or feel uncomfortable? Why?

Chapter Three

Take a breath

It all starts with taking a long slow breath in through the nose, exhale slowly, then repeat.

Great, you made it through the heavy science! Sorry, but there's a bit more on physiology and chemistry. I recognise how ridiculous it sounds that I'm going to explain *how we should breathe*. Of course, we all breathe, but do we do it well? When you are relaxed your body breathes without giving it conscious thought. But what happens to your breath when you activate your trauma response? What happens to your body when your flight-fight-freeze stress response is activated? What I see every day in the clinic are clients who have become anxious, meerkat look-alikes!

It's important to understand that breath keeps you alive and sustains your resilience resources when you're triggered by that feisty mountain lion. You can use your breath as the primary tool for commencing the sedation of your trauma response and changing your trauma tale.

In this chapter I'll outline some simple ways you can practise detaching from your subconscious flight-fight-freeze response and unwind that internal tension; you know, when you feel like you're knotted into a pretzel. It's time to calm your farm and ditch looking like a frazzled, strung-out meerkat that has been doing the tango with the African savannah mountain lion!

I'll talk about how I've used a combination of breathing techniques to overcome massive anxiety during my breast cancer experience. These include various meditation techniques and Wim Hof's breathing and cold therapy techniques. First, let's explore the biology of breath.

You may not realise this but you don't need to be a yogi or meditation guru to learn how to dial down your survival switch behaviours. It might surprise you to learn that you can use your breath to distract the internal monkey mind and mental chatter and learn how to relax your body, all with purposeful breath.

Biology of breath

Do you know how your body systems work to operate normal breathing? You breathe in air, your lungs expand and there is an exchange of oxygen between the lungs and your blood. As you breathe in, your diaphragm should move downwards through into your belly. With each breath, the diaphragm movement pumps your intestines, which allows for expulsion of toxins. With each breath, your heart pumps oxygenated nutrient-rich blood throughout the body.

I've already covered how your sympathetic nervous system takes over when you become triggered. This stress-based response transfers your body from a state of *rest and digest* into *flight or fight*. This neurological shift affects the way you breathe. You migrate unconsciously to a shallow breath, which allows the body to hyperventilate and maximise oxygen intake. The increased oxygen is then used to prime the movement muscles, such as your legs, so that you can run.

Dr Wayne Todd, a chiropractor and author of *SD protocol: Achieve greater health by learning to balance your physical, chemical and emotional wellbeing*, outlines several ways a person can activate sympathetic dominance or overactivation of the sympathetic nervous system. You don't always need trauma to drive this defensive reaction. You can initiate sympathetic activation or flight-fight-freeze from something as simple as unhealthy posture! Did you just sit up straight?

Todd emphasises the need to correct posture when your shoulders are rounded or your head is dropped forward. Todd claims that these two postures can too easily activate a tipping point, which accelerates sympathetic wind-up: a flight-fight-freeze or survival switch response.

Back to your biology! From a structural perspective, rounded shoulders decrease your air intake capacity. Go on, try that now. Throw your shoulders back and take a big deep breath. Now hunch your shoulders forward and repeat the deep breath. Different, isn't it?

The neural messages from the joints to the brain highlight structural stress that all is not well: we're not getting enough oxygen. The result is that the nerve cells receive less oxygen and don't work optimally, which affects your brain integration and overall stability. Think of a time when you lost your kid at the supermarket or came close to having a car accident. You felt tight in the chest and were panting like a meerkat being stalked by a mountain lion on the savannah, right? The fright of the near miss in the car causes our shoulders to round into a defensive position.

I can remember taking part in karate and boxing tournaments as a kid and watching people shrink into themselves to create a *fight stance*. I now know that, neurologically, my opponents were actively utilising their sympathetic nervous system or flight-fight-freeze response to become ready to strike out in defence. In this position you can only breathe to about 80% capacity, therefore you must breathe shallow and fast to get sufficient oxygen just to maintain brain integration.

When you're in that trauma response state of flight or fight, you reduce the downward movement of the diaphragm and the elimination of toxins from your body. You might not know this, but your large intestine becomes the last organ of your body to process emotions! You literally become full of your own shit. For example, when you can't look at your emotional or mental issues that trigger your old trauma response, the consequence is that your body doesn't process faeces. Your bowel is programmed to eliminate whatever it can when stressed; your shit literally runs through you.

I call this phenomenon *monkey-bum*, medically known as diarrhoea. Conversely, if you're big on overanalysing your issues, your body holds on to your shit, which uses an incredible amount of mental energy and you make yourself constipated by hanging on to all those thoughts swirling around inside your head; I know, 'Eeewwww!'

From an endocrinal or hormonal perspective, shallow breathing and activation of your sympathetic nervous system have a negative effect on other internal systems. There is a flow-on effect to your cardiovascular, endocrine, immunity and digestive systems. These systems are all operated by your parasympathetic *rest-digest* nervous system and purposeful breaths.

When you can connect with yourself and recognise how you feel, how rested and calm you are or are not, you can then consciously empower yourself to take action and make changes. Your body is the absolute best barometer to measure how you feel. You can return yourself to an internal place of calm and feeling great again with purposeful breath.

WHEN YOU RECOGNISE HOW YOU FEEL YOU CAN RESUME YOUR INTERNAL BALANCE BECAUSE YOU'RE CONNECTED WITH YOUR OWN, INTERNAL FEEL-GOOD BAROMETER.

Therefore, understanding how your body works means you can consciously dial down your trauma response survival switch. Connecting with your body and understanding how to use your breath enables you to become your own guru and roar.

In my experience, at the height of my PTSD, hot mess phase, I found five key things that worked for me in combination:

1. **Intuitive guided meditation**

    I myself really struggled to sit and meditate without my mind interfering with my calm state. I valued having someone hold space for me, which made me feel safe and not alone.

Using guided meditation, I was directed through an experience that I knew I would feel secure with from the outset. I could develop trust in the simple process and the practitioner. This guided experience also provided me with options, such as emergency exits and to be in charge of what I visualised so that I could always feel like I was in a safe, calm place.

This technique enabled me to deeply relax my body, allowing me to correct my posture and release pain from my upper chest and neck. Relaxing these parts of my body enabled me to feel like I could slow down and breathe deeply, to feel inherently safe. I particularly enjoy the energy of partaking in group guided meditation; there's just something so powerfully magical when women come together. It's one of my favourite services that I now offer.

2. Counting meditation 

This was fabulous when I felt triggered, heightened, panicked or breathless. I found this technique very useful when I'd activated my anxiety-based, raw reaction survival switch, shallow breathing; just think panicked meerkat bolting into a tunnel in the African savannah with a mountain lion only a claw away. I always knew when this switch had been flicked on because I looked like a strung-out meerkat hyperventilating and in desperate need for a brown paper bag! Let me assure you, this wasn't my sexiest look. For me, being a practitioner, this was downright embarrassing.

The counting meditation gave me conscious evidence that whilst the triggers of my survival switching couldn't be controlled immediately in that stress moment, I could breathe to help calm myself. I found this incredibly empowering. The exercise involved breathing in and counting to four, holding my breath for a count of two and then slowly releasing my breath for a count of six, and then repeating this process for approximately two minutes.

The counting became a pleasant distraction from whatever was stressing me out. Sometimes, I'll acknowledge, I didn't know what the trigger was and I just felt anxious. This exercise also enabled me to correct my posture so I could maintain an extended, deep breath.

This is an exceptionally good tool for when I feel initially triggered, like driving in peak hour traffic, attending oncology treatments and being cannulised, or the commencement of scans where I'm inside another machine. It doesn't relax me so much that I want to sleep, but it cuts the crap of that heightened anxious feeling.

3. Chanting mantras 

Now, I will not lie, I was extremely skeptical about this exercise when I first heard about it, however, I was in such a frayed, hot mess state I had nothing to lose except anxiety.

My meditation teacher spoke of the energy of sound vibrations and how sound can heal at a cellular level. As a kinesiology practitioner, I'd learnt about the benefits of energy vibrations but never appreciated the direct experience. I'll discuss energy more in the next chapter.

My teacher cross-referenced the scientific research and photographs taken of water molecules by Dr Emoto, who researched positive words being placed on Petri dishes containing water. After several days, the microscopic view of the structure of the water molecule changed to a beautiful, crystalline structure. Dr Emoto's research also included writing negative words on the

Petri dishes of water. After several days the microscopic view of the water molecules appeared toxic and broken.

I wanted to achieve that internal state of being a happy, bright and sparkly crystal! Who doesn't, right? I will admit I started with a very basic 'Ohm' but got bored quickly. I can't explain why I pursued this. Once again spirit nudged me to continue trying this method until it worked.

After researching options on YouTube and liaising with my meditation teacher, I found a mantra that resonated with me. I discovered the *om namah shivaya*, which loosely translates as *universal consciousness is one*. Sounds like a mouthful, right? I struggled to get the knack of this on my own and retreated to YouTube for a chanting guide and this turned out to be the key to my success. Basically, the guide shows how to use your breath to sound out the syllables of the words and then you replicate the chant. Sounds easy, but it's physically and mentally demanding.

What I discovered was that the chant forced me to do several things, primarily not to focus on my anxiety. First, I had to focus intently on the sound made for each syllable to replicate it. I had to concentrate on the use of my abdominal muscles and how I breathed. I had to change how I inhaled, including the speed, which allowed me to explore the extension of time I could hold a particular tonal note with my breath. This exercise also forced me to correct my posture to ensure I could open my chest up to get the breath I needed.

Using a guided chant, whereby the instructor performed the chant and then you copy, left time for me to follow to the same timing. It stunned me that after repeating a mantra for 108 times, which took about 20 minutes, I was no longer panicked. I was no longer in a heightened raw reaction state. And any tension that I had been holding in my body had disappeared.

I was completely gobsmacked and have since saved to my YouTube favourites for any time the universe throws me a curveball that makes my knees wobble. Other than having a kinesiology balance or psychology therapy session, this is my number one tool I use to kick anxiety square in the nuts. A single chanting session makes anxiety disappear so that I can sleep and function. It's now my go-to tool for when I have to do any form of enclosed imaging or screening appointment, which is a big trigger for me.

4. Dawn nature immersion walk

Psychotherapist and researcher Kelly A Turner, author of *Radical remission: Surviving cancer against all odds: The nine key factors that can make a real difference*, related a story of Shin Terayama who recovered from cancer. Whilst he was in hospital, after receiving intense chemotherapy, his sense of smell and taste were severely affected. One night he escaped the smell of the hospital ward and took himself to the roof to get fresh air. He later realised after finishing his chemotherapy he was hypersensitive to smell and was constantly drawn to places where there was fresh air to cleanse his sense of smell. He realised through a series of experiments at home that oxygen levels are increased 42 minutes before the sunrise.

The process of photosynthesis within the leaves of plants transforms carbon dioxide to oxygen. Shin combined the practice of immense gratitude for waking each day with a deep breathing, chanting practice at dawn, relishing the eventual warmth of a new day's sunlight. With each breath out he would make a sound, whilst touching various parts of his body and noting where the sound changed. In fact, he was activating his chakra system and completing his own healing with the use of breathing elevated oxygen levels with chanting sounds and gratitude.

I'm a science nerd and love a bit of research. I'm an environmental industrial chemist by trade, so I love my experiments. Using the warmth of early summer mornings and daylight savings time, during my recovery from multiple surgeries and oncology treatments, I organised a 'mate-date' walk every morning. Naturally, during our chat and trot time we discussed Shin's experiment and were both stunned that our ability to walk and talk was different during that early morning time of blue to pink light, right at dawn. Every day the air tasted cleaner; it was like we were sitting in an oxygen tank that primed our body for the day. Walking at this time of the day left us feeling energised. It was incredible.

Walking outside serves many purposes, like exposing our body to UV light to create vitamin D. As we move at a pace where we can just maintain a conversation whilst briskly walking, we create endorphins. Walking also pumps freshly oxygenated blood around our body, flushing the lymphatic system. This is one of my mandatory, maintenance exercises that I try to complete daily. In my circumstances, after so much reconstructive surgery, my connective tissue easily gets stiff and walking is fabulous to manage pain.

5. Wim Hof's (the Iceman) breathing exercise

Most would doubt the power of introducing cold showers with a simple breathing technique to achieve a change in as little as 10 days, as proclaimed by Wim Hof. I tried his breath technique first, followed by the cold immersion showers. I now use this technique as ongoing daily support before performing each physiotherapy rehabilitation exercise regime. Using Hof's breathing technique enables me to complete all the tasks without pain and at greater capacity. I added cold showers to my morning routine and now thoroughly enjoy starting my day by incorporating his breathing technique into my morning meditation routine, followed by a cold shower. It's one of the better alternatives to caffeine I've ever experienced.

It's common to experience objection or doubts about how powerful the use of breath is, until you experiment and understand the importance it plays in keeping you calm and sedating your raw reaction trauma response. Since the height of my PTSD symptoms, my daily routine has transformed. I now live a life that is much slower paced and purposeful. My self-care regime is extensive. I get the bonus of my daily connection with my friend as we 'mate-date' most mornings and get our oxygen fix. I've shared my favourite breathing exercises and recommend you find what works for you.

Mountain lion tamer tips to learn to breathe purposefully

How do you improve your purposeful breath?

1. Maintain good posture.

2. Try relaxation yoga.

3. Belly breathing.

    a. Place one hand on your chest, the other hand on your belly.

    b. Breathe deeply and allow the initial rise of your chest.

    c. Now concentrate and continue slow deep breaths until you can push your belly out whilst keeping your chest still.

4. Intuitive guided meditation.

    a. Take a class or listen online and allow someone to guide you through a safe, relaxing guided meditation experience.

    b. Start with something simple like breathing for relaxation for just a couple of minutes until you get the hang of the process. Remember to allow your thoughts to come and go.

5. Counting meditation.

    a. Sit or lie somewhere comfortable and quiet.

    b. Breathe in for a count of four.

    c. Breathe out for a count of four.

    d. Repeat for six breaths.

    e. Now try introducing a pause between the in and out breath or breathe for a count of five to six.

6. Chanting mantras.

    a. At the end of each day, I use a chant which forces my body to hold a sound note.

    b. Try a guided chant to start the process – this will support you to find the correct breathing rhythm.

7. Take nature immersion walks.

8. Explore Wim Hof's breathing method.

    a. Watch his YouTube video first to see if this aligns to your current needs and whether this is the right action for you.

The barrier to starting anything is always ensuring you feel safe. The second aspect to address is your motivation to see you through to the end of the exercise, as well as then being able to repeat the process. I always try something new for at least two weeks to allow myself to observe where any struggle arises and deal with it. What arises in terms of avoidance, discomfort or the shenpa is the lesson waiting to be learnt. The struggle therefore becomes a gem and something to look forward to.

You gain more enthusiasm by repeating a new process and mastering it. You also develop muscle memory for your conscious breath when you practise these activities repeatedly over at least a week. Grant yourself permission to consciously connect to how you're feeling. Allow yourself a moment or two of reflection to determine what works for you. This reflection can be one of the best gifts for self. After all, this is your healing journey.

Of course, there are exceptions, especially implementing Wim Hof's technique and he is the first to point them out together with the science. The exception is associated with any pre-existing medical conditions like asthma, lung disease or recovering from an illness. For these conditions, you should liaise with your medical practitioner for clearance or approval. There's an obvious, serious mental health condition like schizophrenia, medicated anxiety or depression whereby, if you're trying anything new, it should be done with the supervision, not just approval, of your qualified physician.

Remember, always consult your regular physician if you've got any concerns or questions regarding your ability to breathe freely. There's an added exception that I use in my own clinical practice for those who run deep-seated fear patterns or for those people for whom trying anything new causes them even more panic and anxiety. You'll probably benefit from commencing something like Wim Hof's exercises under the supervision of a trained professional. This is so the qualified expert can guide you through the fear to be able to enjoy the experience.

Become your own guru

This section introduces the neuro-emotional biology of breath. It's funny, you know, our brain is a sexy beast and according to *New Scientist* journal's 'Introduction: The human brain', it weighs 1.4 kilograms and comprises an estimated one hundred billion mountain lion neuron cells. Your grey matter is responsible for driving your emotional response, your mental thoughts and processes, including behaviour, as well as coordinating the movement of your body.

Believe it or not, all this emotional stuff is driven by the jelly between your ears: your neurons, their pathways and how well these neural tracts remain integrated during times of stress! And you're back to how your trauma tale influences your sense of wellbeing!

Your brain waves can cause you to feel like you have run out of breath based on how and when your survival switch is activated. Brain waves change with emotions and survival switching. This is because of the threat assessment undertaken by the amygdala as I have discussed earlier in chapter two.

The speed of brain waves changes depending on how your brain is functioning, for example:

- *Delta waves* are slow and of low frequency and deeply penetrate the brain. Delta waves occur during your dreamless sleep and meditation and they are highly beneficial for deep healing. Your breathing is deep and cyclical here.

- *Theta waves* are the gateway to your learning, memory, and intuition. Theta waves operate when you're in that twilight state as you drift off to sleep or enter a deep meditation. It's also where you hold all your stuff like over-emotions and fears. Your breath here fluctuates and slows down, introducing a slow, deep breath now and then, until a deep relaxation sigh is often uttered.

HUMAN BRAIN WAVES

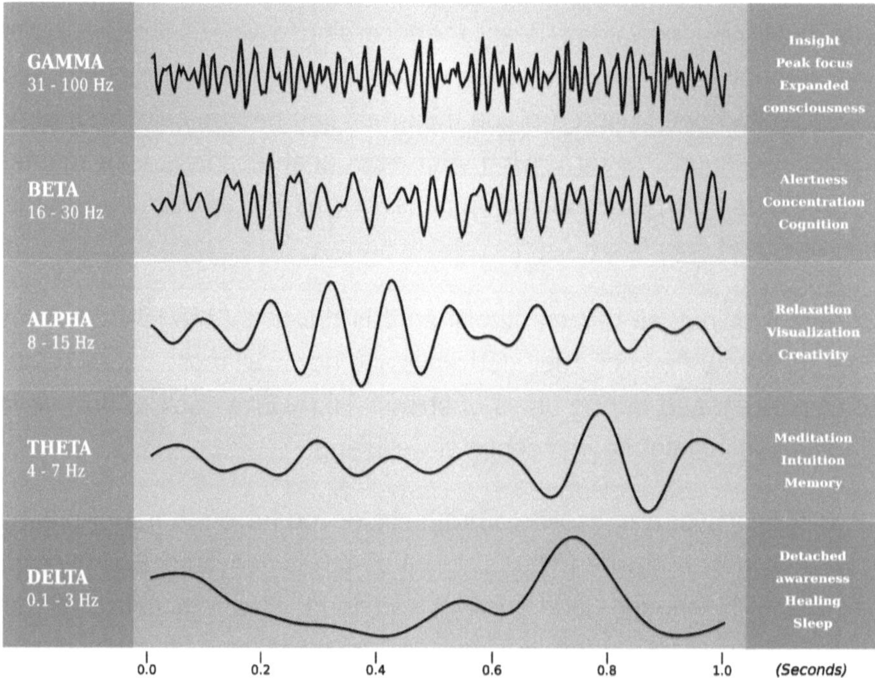

- *Alpha waves* are your natural resting state of the brain, supporting mental coordination, calmness, alertness and learning. Breath here should be stable but will change based on the environment you are in and the sensory information flooding the brain.

- *Beta waves* dominate your waking state of consciousness and are engaged in fast activities of problem-solving and decision-making. This is where your breath matches what you are thinking and aligns to the pace of life. Fast life, rapid and shallow breaths follow. Therefore, you can feel exhausted after a busy day.

- *Gamma waves* are those high frequency waves linked with universal love and expanded consciousness. Originally it was thought gamma waves could not be consciously influenced, however research has shown that meditation and practices of mindfulness can connect you back to proactively activating your gamma wave function. The breath is quite purposeful, even and deep here. The shoulders are back, your diaphragm is relaxed.

Referencing brain waves, you can see that the body operates cyclically during a 24-hour period. This is called the *circadian rhythm* and it's your body's internal clock, running in the background to carry out essential functions and processes. During the day, your circadian rhythms enable you to get out of bed and function, being part of the sleep-wake cycle. Now, imagine how stress can interfere with your ability to sleep deeply and therefore activate delta waves to restore brain function for the next day.

Your brain operates in an integrated fashion, incorporating both logic and emotional functioning. So, imagine what happens when you experience stress over a long period or a trauma? Your trauma tale's raw reaction *to* survival switching turns off your brain's ability to remain integrated. The survival-behavioural program is activated and sleep patterns are interrupted, which reduces relaxation of the entire body. This is often where the seed of that panic attack breathing is planted by your unresolved, raw reaction trauma tale that became a habit.

When your brain waves are interrupted by switching, your circadian rhythm is also disturbed. Your brain function becomes chaotic and switches to simple survival mode. On a subconscious level the brain's operational capacity isn't operating a program for procreation, creativity or relaxation. When in survival, your brain is running the pattern, 'What is the bare minimum I need to do to get through this shit festival?' The brain loves repetition. Therefore, rerunning the survival program is simple and easy for the brain because it bypasses the

- frontal cortex where the solution-oriented thinking occurs
- neocortex at the top of the brain where your 'big girl pants' thinking happens.

This path of least resistance to survival reinforces our sensation of raw reactions with shallow breathing. This creates the shenpa itch of discomfort of why you feel stressed and reactive. Repeat this pattern for over two weeks and you've got yourself a subconscious habit.

So, the practice of mindfulness or being purposeful becomes such a healing modality all on its own.

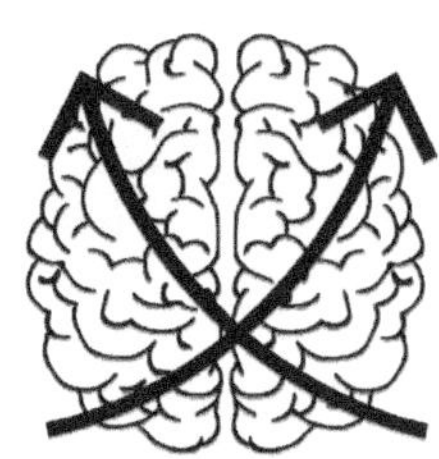

Side to side

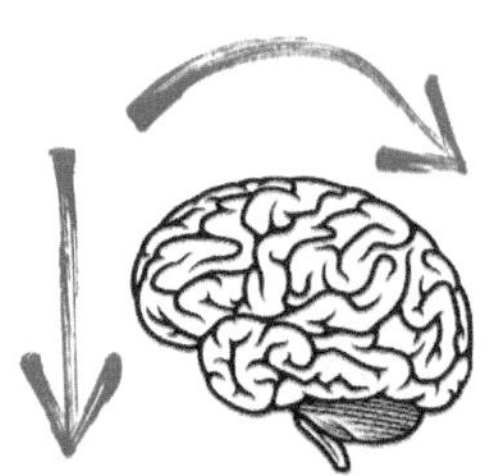

Front to back and top to bottom

So, what is mindfulness?

The Mayo Clinic defines mindfulness as 'a mental state of being whereby you can focus your attention on the present moment called now'. It's a place within yourself whereby you can calmly acknowledge and accept your feelings and thoughts and connect with your bodily sensations. In my experience, the use of breath to activate mindfulness is a superpower; bold statement, I know. But when you are present with yourself, you can acknowledge what is going on in that moment. I'll talk more about this in chapter six, but for now let's remain focused on how to harness your breath further.

OUR BREATH IS ONE OF THE MOST BASIC, POWERFUL WAYS TO ACTIVATE AND PRACTICE MINDFULNESS AND RESTORE CALM TO AN INTERNAL STORM.

You can amplify the power of your breath with mantras. A mantra is a positive quote that inspires you to take action. Let me be clear: when you're amid your trauma tale raw state, the only action you may take is a deep breath and that's okay, honey. Breathing is important. Consciously and purposefully deep breathing is golden.

Mantras are spoken using your external voice because you are setting an intention for yourself to take action. For example, on your inward breath state, 'I am' and on your outward breath state your mantra. Here's one I use every day: 'I am surrendering to ordinary thinking.'

Ordinary thinking is the headspace that makes your days blur together. It's living with the expectation that your to-do list can be completed or that if you do everything life will be perfect. Let me call *bullshit* on all of it. Ordinary thinking is for muggles who are only existing in their mundane, stressful life. Laying down the need to please anyone but yourself is the action of surrender, which can be achieved with breath. Inhaling deeply and slowly, counting to five, is often all you need to draw your attention inwards from the drama of the world outside of you. It is from this moment of inward perspective that you become your own guru.

To combat that raw reaction of your trauma response, mindful breathing can be successfully used as the simplistic basic tool to turn off or wind back the dial of your survival switch. You don't need to become a Buddhist monk who lives in a cave and meditates for years on end to achieve enough relaxation to heal. You can simply use and purposefully connect to your breath to achieve the same result in a moment of stress. The more often you allow yourself to notice your raw reaction, take a breath and remain present, the easier it is to acknowledge what is going on and seek support.

The key tool I used during my breast cancer experience and recovering from PTSD was using the power of intention with breath. I always aim to remain in the present moment, but I'm human and like everyone else have triggers. That said, I've become my own guru and allow my breath to get me back to present time. Therefore, I've provided many mantra and quote options in this book, so that you too have the choice and can attempt to resonate with something that empowers you to change in your life.

An example of using purposeful breath is demonstrated by the world record-breaker Wim Hof, nicknamed the Iceman for his ability to break world records in ice-bathing and breath-holding. He is also the author of *The Wim Hof method: Activate your potential, transcend your limits*. Hof presents several techniques, which I've found exceptionally beneficial. He presents utilising a simple breathing technique with cold therapy to reset the survival switch of your sympathetic nervous system and how it dominates you and places you in a state of survival.

An objection or doubt arises about Wim Hof's method, and I constantly hear this from my own clients in practice who say, 'I've tried to meditate and it's too hard' or 'I can't concentrate when I'm meditating and therefore it's too hard.' My response is always that meditation is designed to place you in the time zone of now rather than empty your head. Thoughts and feelings are meant to come and go when you're meditating and you're meant to relax enough to allow that to happen.

There is a misperception that you should feel like and become like a guru during and after meditation. This just isn't the case. I constantly reiterate to my meditation class participants that it is simply a relaxation tool and one I use and prescribe as homework for my clinical clients. Society paints such an illusionary and unrealistic picture that meditation will be a quick fix.

Let me be very clear: a consistent meditation practice will support you to sedate your fired-up, scaredy-cat nervous system to 'calm the fuck down'. A single session might make you feel okay in the moment but it won't last until you deal with your survival switch, your shenpa.

Meditation is such a useful tool because survival switching takes you out of your own flow of life and disconnects you from this present moment, now time zone. Survival switching projects you into either the past or the future and usually with a shenpa hook that is fear-based.

Most people don't know how to meditate or what meditation is and would greatly benefit from supervision, for example, a guided meditation. A useful starting block is meditation with purposeful breath and this is an act of submitting back into yourself. Meditation with breath enables you to release or detach from the outside world and everything going on outside of you. It's an active, rapid connection back into your heart space, where all your innate wisdom resides. Successful meditation brings you into the present moment, allowing thoughts to come and go. Repeating this process regularly, like every day, supports you to use purposeful breath to reset your circadian rhythm and normal brainwave patterns so that you can truly relax and recuperate.

There are exceptions to attempting meditation by yourself. When I went looking for documented, scientific research pertaining to unwanted side effects of meditation and mindful breath, I struggled to find any. In my clinical experience, there is the obvious caution for those diagnosed with serious mental health conditions like schizophrenia, especially when unstable, or bipolar, when having an unmanaged high or low. These conditions require supervision with your medical practitioner to begin any new activity to ensure no adverse or unwanted side effects occur.

Warning! If you have deep-seated fear patterns, where attempting anything new or change pushes your buttons, I strongly advise you to undertake this practice with supervision and a trained meditation instructor.

 **Mountain lion tamer tip to become your own guru**

1. Emergency moment – breathe when you are triggered.

2. Remove yourself from a stressful situation.

3. Go somewhere quiet and private like the toilet.

4. Breathe in deeply and count to ten, breathe out with a *whoosh*.

5. As you breathe in tell yourself, 'In this moment I am safe.'

6. Try guided meditation with variations.

7. Counting four by four breaths.

8. Identify places and spaces where you feel safe to just be your authentic self without having to put on a show for others.

9. Dance to your favourite music allowing your body to move freely, noticing how your breath has changed after shaking your groove thing.

10. Start to observe your breath and posture.

Pick one action that resonates with you and try it for a week, taking notice on which days the technique you chose is most valuable for you and notice when it's not. Every day will be different and you may require a different tool. This is another reason why I've created a variety of actions for you to identify what is the best fit for you. Consciously connecting with what makes you feel good enables you to become your own guru.

Distract the internal monkey

When you become consciously aware that you have activated the survival switch, you recognise that your breath has sped up and become quite shallow, almost to the point of hyperventilation. For some, this can feel like tightness across the chest, others identify it as panic. Just think of a stressed-out meerkat breathing rapidly in and out; is that you?

When you detach from your heart space, that place within you where all your innate wisdom and love energy resides, you go up into your head and your mind gets chatty. This creates a chaotic mental response and it feeds the energy of fear, as well as 'but-what-if', 'shoulda', 'coulda' and 'woulda' questions. This is how internal overanalysis begins. I call it *monkey chatter*. The incessant questioning, overanalysing and getting yourself wrapped up into a hot mess, like a salty pretzel, leaves you feeling quite vulnerable and often short of breath.

Mindless *monkey chatter* causes you to become distracted very easily. It throws you out of the present moment and into a different time zone: either the past where you overanalyse what you could have, should have or would have done differently, or the mindless *monkey chatter* that throws you into the future with questions such as, 'but what if this happens, what if that happens?' This is where the fear of uncertainty and the fear of the unknown arise.

When you're not 'in the now' or present moment, you can become fear driven. There is very little internal love for self because you are not grounded in the energy of your heart space or using gamma brain waves. When you aren't present, you're simply running a survival program operated from alpha brain waves and the amygdala undertaking a threat response. Symptoms of *monkey chatter* can look and feel like anxiety and panic, feelings of being out of control or needing control, or fear.

Monkey chatter makes you feel bonkers.

It's important to understand and remain aware of when your mind has taken over from your heart. Connecting with your breath is an extremely powerful tool to use consciously to reset your survival switch and put you back into a place of rest and digest, rather than becoming stuck once again in your trauma response.

A ten-second breath can often support you to pause and not overreact or step out of external drama. That same breath can often give you time to realise you have been triggered and not invest in what's going on around you. When you first start this activity of a ten-second breath you may even like to physically step back to remind your brain you're not under threat from the mountain lion in the fridge, it's just an old trigger that has arisen for you to now deal with. You can use the simple breathing technique of counting to ten to trick your monkey mind into submission and return to a deeper breath, which sedates the nervous system.

When I first started working with Jackson, his doctor wanted to medicate him to control his panic attacks, anxiety and depression. During each session, I introduced breathing techniques with the aid of short meditation recordings so he had homework to practise the techniques. Each time we identified safe places and then utilised guided breath meditations to reintroduce mindful breathing techniques to override his trauma response.

I began this process using a visualisation technique to enable Jackson to safely reconnect into his heart space with meditative breath. He gained enormous confidence quickly and was able to readily implement the homework.

As our work progressed over several months, Jackson was able to visualise safely connecting with an aspect of his personality: his inner child, who had been molested. Until this point, Jackson had never felt safe enough to speak up about this period of his life where the assaults were frequent. Jackson's anxiety returned during the session with a vengeance.

It's in moments like these that I'm grateful for my spiritual experiences and my own personal journey work I've done, paired with my training. At this point, where Jackson felt incredibly vulnerable, I empowered the adult version of Jackson with permission. I told him to breathe and when his panic subsided, I told him to parent the younger version of himself. I gave him permission to make that younger version of himself feel safe.

Using meditation, I could direct Jackson as an adult to breathe and he later advised that he watched his inner child slow his breathing down. As the adult he was able to reach out his hand to the child and then embrace the child. He was then able to take the child in his arms, stand and walk out of the room where he had been repeatedly assaulted and take that child to a safe place.

The use of purposeful breath sedated Jackson's survival switch. The meditation provided Jackson with access to his creative mind to visualise an old and extremely painful memory that had continued to affect his behaviour twenty years later. At the completion of that session, Jackson's tears were of happiness. He reported finally feeling calm and free of the extreme anger he had been experiencing.

Recognise when your chatty mind monkey enables you to consciously calm yourself using your preferred breathing techniques.

Wrap-up

So far, I've explained Western science and how the brain and body work biologically, but there's another aspect to understand: the way energy influences your ability to heal from a trauma experience. That's coming up in the next chapter. Perhaps now you'll take moments to continue checking your posture throughout the day. Perhaps you'll enjoy an extended sigh and celebrate feeling calm and relaxed.

Mountain lion tamer affirmations to support purposeful breath

Biology of breath

1. With each breath I feel myself calm and relax.

2. I breathe the energy of change.

3. My breath flows easily and deeply, nourishing my body, mind and soul.

Be your own guru

4. With each breath I ground myself into the now.

5. Purposeful breath gives me purpose and strength to calm.

6. With each purposeful breath I am brought back into the present moment.

Distract the internal monkey

7. I am open to change.

8. I look inward for my answers.

9. I am safe to internally explore to find the answers I seek.

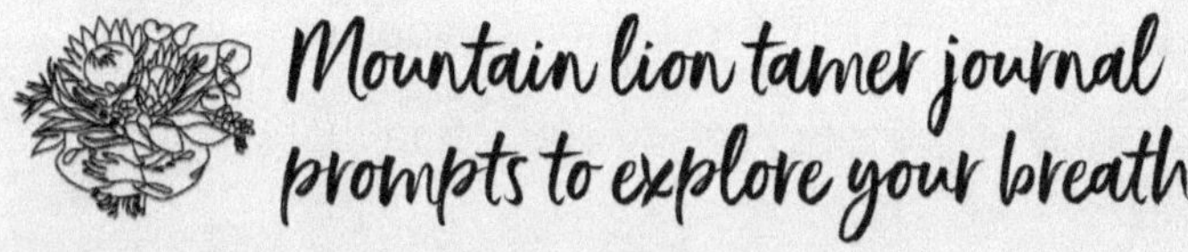 *Mountain lion tamer journal prompts to explore your breath*

Biology of breath

1. When I experience stress, the awareness I have about my lungs, chest and breathing is…

2. What would my life be like if I could breathe as if I already had the ability to take control?

3. What method enables me to breathe and move from survival to thriving in my life?

4. What might my life be if with each breath I felt safe in my space?

Be your own guru

5. If I were to be totally honest with myself right now and gift myself permission to gently express whilst taking purposeful breaths

   a. Can I accept this situation right now? If not, what aspect is creating a hook and trapping me in the pattern of not letting go?

   b. Do I really need to understand the story of this traumatic experience right now, or can I gift myself permission to simply acknowledge it happened and move on?

   c. If you need to understand, commence gentle exploration with this question, 'What is the gift I could learn about myself from having had this experience?'

6. Whilst practising mindful breathing ask yourself

    a. Is there an experience inside your head that won't go away?

    b. What is it? Why does it haunt me?

    c. Does this story need an ending?

    d. Explore your story in your journal and write a positive ending to the story. Allow each breath to take you through the energy of the story you've been holding on to.

    e. What could you let go of or pause to not feel exhausted by maintaining the patterns developed because of your experience?

Distract the internal monkey

7. Choose one of these prompts after several minutes of mindful breathing and free-write for five minutes. If the topic takes off, stay with it until you reach a point of completion. If the writing seems stuck, choose another prompt. Revise it if needed.

    a. I have never talked about this…

    b. The hardest lie I ever told myself was…

    c. The way it really was…

    d. It is dangerous to…

    e. This story is hidden in a box in the back of my mind. It begins with…

8. What wisdom did you gain from this journal exercise?

    a. Were you able to make connection with your breath and continue to remain in a calm space?

Everything is energy

Everything requires energy to function. When the energy doesn't flow strongly, is interrupted or even blocked, you experience internal chaos.

In this chapter, I summarise how energy plays a role in your ability to create a stable foundation for life. I refer to this as being *centred*, within yourself. When you're centered, your energy flows and this is everything to be able to live harmoniously. We all migrate through life experiencing challenges. Some overcome them, some don't.

When you experience a trauma, it can feel like it has pushed you off-kilter and, speaking from personal experience, this feels horrendous. Without a stable foundation, you feel raw and can't meet your human need for security. When you are disconnected from your internal resilience resources, everything in life feels like a battle that must be fought.

There are a variety of energetic medicine concepts commonly used by modern day practitioners to restore balance to energetic systems interrupted by trauma. I routinely discuss these energetic medicine concepts with my clients because they are not understood for recovery from trauma.

So far, I've thrown a lot of Western science your way, which describes only one aspect of your trauma tale. Let's balance the scales by introducing concepts from Eastern energy modalities, their energetic medicine principles and their influence on your trauma responses. With that in mind, allow me to introduce you to some traditional Chinese medicine with specific reference to meridian theory.

Everything in nature and life itself requires energy to function. It comes in a variety of formats and being in a grounded state allows us to connect to that energy. The *New Scientist* journal defines quantum physics as, 'how everything in life works: the best description we have of the nature of the particles that make up matter and the forces with which they interact. Quantum physics underlies how atoms work and so why chemistry and biology work as they do.'

Let's skip the boring science lecture and simply focus on this: humans aren't just physical, emotional, or mental energies. Your internal systems do not operate as separate entities. Your bodies are comprised of cellular based systems. To function, internal and external forces energetically drive your cellular systems. I can almost hear your eyes rolling into the back of your head! A trauma tale can affect any of these energy systems and jeopardise the ability of the body to function optimally.

JUST LIKE MONEY, EVERYTHING IN NATURE RELIES UPON ENERGY THAT FLOWS RATHER THAN STAGNATING.

A traumatic experience can generate internal chaos that feels like bone-tired exhaustion which sleep won't resolve. Your mental energy becomes unbalanced and suddenly life comprises problems that get stuck on a merry-go-round inside your head. Emotional energy disturbance can be experienced as a never-ending sadness or negative outlook on life.

Energetic disturbances can even feel like insurmountable anxiety or nonprescriptive pain for which there is no apparent cause. Clients have often reported to me they feel like there is a rave party going on inside their body where everyone has been dancing for hours and dropping acid. How on earth can you meet your human need for certainty and security in internal chaos?

Dare I say it: chaotic energy can leave you feeling like a pile of stinky 'poo'. Let's be honest though, disturbance in your energy systems has a cascade effect on many of your systems and energetic fields, and if avoided it leads to shenpa. It leaves you feeling uncomfortable.

Picture finding a mountain lion inside your fridge. If you're lucky and your resilience is high, after you've slammed the fridge door, having sat somewhere quiet as the adrenaline faded, you're left feeling exhausted and overwhelmed, wondering what the hell just happened. If your energy systems are chaotic (for whatever reason), you as the pile of 'poo' have now been stomped flat and smeared over the floor. Now your 'shit' stinks and has spread to the point you can't step over or around it anymore. You can no longer avoid it. Your shit is everywhere! Using the analogy of being a tree, your roots that have previously grounded you are now exposed. You're vulnerable and this is what I mean by raw.

WE DON'T VIEW OURSELVES AS A VAST NETWORK OF CELLS AND MOLECULES, LET ALONE AN INTERACTING WEB OF PARTICLES, MATTER AND ENERGY WAVES THAT SHOULD COEXIST HARMONIOUSLY WITHIN THE UNIVERSE.

Trauma interferes with your outward focus, and you can become stuck and internally directed. You lose your reference to the external world, rather than viewing yourself as an infinite series of interconnected relationships within and beyond yourself.

When I explain the various energetic systems and how disturbances to the energy fields may be experienced, some clients can very much feel like they are walking onto the set of the *Matrix* without meeting Neo (a.k.a. Keanu Reeves). Wrap your thinking around the concept that you're a unique speckle of holographic energy within the cosmos. Embracing yourself as a cosmic star requires you to align to everything around you to thrive. It's pretty humbling.

Chakras – be a DJ and spin your unique soundtrack

One of the more commonly known energy systems is based on the Indian energy vortices called *chakras* or *energy-wheels*. My kinesiology studies focused on the seven main chakras between the base of the spine and top of the head, in which energy flows in and out of your body. You've probably heard that chakras are colour-based energy centres and not thought twice about it. What you probably don't know is that each chakra corresponds to various nerve bundles of major organs and their body systems, such as digestion and endocrine systems, as well as your emotional and physical wellbeing.

Think of your chakras as an energy system that functions as a song that can harmonise with anything in nature; if there is stress within one component of your unique music, sound, vibration or beat, it can feel like the alignment to your internal harmony is off. Does this make sense? You meet your human need for connection and security, feel tethered to your ability to heal as well as to your *higher self,* your true purpose, when your chakra energy systems are balanced.

CHAKRAS ARE THE ENERGETIC MAP TO OUR DIVINE SONG FOR LIFE

Our chakra system directs energy into and out of your bodies via our endocrine system (hormonal glands). According to international neuro-anatomy brain integration instructor Jacque Mooney, 'the nervous system uses the nerves to conduct information and the endocrine system mainly uses blood vessels as information channels with direct hormone secretion into the blood system. Each of the chakras operates through an in-body, endocrine gland, which allows outer body chakras to interact with physical body and create change to homeostasis.'

Mooney shares research undertaken by Dr Shafica Karagulla, author of *The chakras and human energy fields,* which incorporated a clairvoyant's assessment of chakras and human body fields and then compared this to a standard medical diagnosis. Dr Karagulla's research highlighted that diseases alter the behaviour of chakras and the way energy moves in and out of the body. Trauma directly impacts the energy flow within the chakra system and the functioning of the body.

Authors Mooney, Massey, Fraser and Brennan all mention that your human energy field is contributed to by the chakra system. Chakras are vortices of energy with energy flowing in and out of each centre, as well as along the spinal column. There are associated relationship traits, emotions and various colours associated with each chakra. Remember that colour has its own vibrational energetic frequency!

What most people don't realise is that the chakra contains the sum of electrical memory of everything that ever happens to us. In his book, *Health building: The conscious art of living well*, Dr Randolph Stone discusses how chakras have their own polarity or electrical charge. Mooney outlines the chakras' charge is different from the electrical conduction within the nervous system and different to the electro-chemical nature of our endocrine or hormonal system. I know I'm banging on about the science but let me pull this all together now for you!

Just like a magnet attracts objects with opposite polarity (electrical charge), or repels objects with the same polarity, chakras operate the same way. The chakras' electrical memory properties can detect energy disturbances around them. Your body can detect energetically someone else's mood before the amygdala can undertake a threat assessment of that someone standing near you, review their body language and then their words. This type of energy is referenced as metaphysics.

If that is hard to digest, use the example of music. As a child of the '80s, I like soft rock and anything with a mellow four-by-four beat where I can understand the lyrics of the song. For me, this type of music has a positive vibrational charge and I can extend my energy outwards. Harnessing my positive energy, I feel confident enough to shake my groove thing in public, much to my daughter's disgust as anyone could be in the checkout line at Kmart these days!

Conversely, my body literally cringes defensively if someone beside me is playing heavy metal music. For me, this is a negatively charge vibrational energy. I feel myself drawing my energy inward, physically shrinking into myself, into that defensive state much like a trauma response. If I listen to this metal music long enough, it activates my survival switch and my need to flee the situation, which moves me to a quieter space.

Now imagine you've had a trauma experience or you're running that raw, reactive survival switch; sensory information like sound, sight, taste and touch can all be triggers, which reactivate the survival switch. Regular or ongoing reactivation of the switch drives the development of habitual, defensive behaviour.

What happens when you listen to sad music? You cry! The music vibration can invoke the release of built-up emotional energy to be expressed. Remember, your body can record this as an electrical memory in the chakra centre, which affects the corresponding organs. The flow-on effect travels to every cell and your memory pathways of the brain. Your amygdala goes bonkers with its threat assessment when any of the miniscule criteria from that experience are activated as being present again. Is it any wonder you feel exhausted after having a good cry? – your whole body is energetically responding!

 **Mountain lion tamer tips to align to your rhythm**

There are a variety of ways to balance your chakra energy system:

1. Yoga poses are fabulous for opening the body's energy centres using stretching and breath.

2. Often you experience a flush of heat or chill off when you shift to an energetic disturbance.

3. Yoga often finishes with a short meditation or rest period whereby you cover yourself with a blanket to allow your internal energy to regroup and restore balance after performing the poses.

4. Sound healing – singing bowls resonate specific tonal frequencies.

5. Chakra colour meditation.

Meridians – get flowing

Traditional Chinese Medicine (TCM) theory originated in the third century and incorporates how a person can bring *heavenly chi* into their body. TCM identified that meridians are the conduit that allows the flow of our vital life force. Meridian-like channels coordinate the information that drives millions of chemical processes, ensuring that the correct information gets to a specific place in the body at the precise time it is required.

The twelve main meridians correspond to the twelve primary organs of the body. Just like with your nervous system and the chakras, when energy flow is disturbed, the function of the meridian system does not perform optimally.

Each meridian has a peak-function period of two hours and a corresponding partner meridian that is ebbing as energy flows throughout the meridian system of the body. Therefore, the meridian system energy cycles over a 24-hour period of a day. What I learnt is that the elemental phases of Chinese medicine are also cyclical and seasonally based in nature.

According to John Kirkwood, author of *The way of the five elements*, fire, earth, metal, water and wood reflect how energy functions within nature.

An elemental cycle represents how you evolve in nature; each element has a relationship with every other element with elements best described as cycles much like the seasons over the course of a year.

Kirkwood expands the concept of elements by referencing the seasons of the year, stating that each season has its own vibrational force. Think about it: we all have a relationship with a particular season or time of the year because of the activity and joy we experience during that period.

The elemental system incorporates different energetic vibrations, which can be expressed not only in nature, but also within our bodies. Each chakra and meridian has an association with a predominant colour, sound, emotion, odour, organ, set of tissues and psychological and spiritual states. Each of these physical components within humans is detecting the energetic frequency via the meridian system, clarifying the information via the note and resonance of the vibration of that energetic information.

When you are in balance of any elemental aspect, this harmony is translated to balanced expression within the organs, tissues, mood, and mindset. If there is disturbance within the meridian system because of a trauma tale, the frequency of information is distorted, energy will not flow optimally.

The benefit of using the energy of the meridian system to correct distortion within the body is that once harmony and balance are restored to a single meridian, that harmony can flow throughout other meridians and body systems. For example, as a complementary therapies practitioner, I work with defusing the emotion of anger and cross-reference the organs and tissues which relate to that emotion. The emotion of anger lives in the liver and gall bladder.

I get it. This all sounds a little fruity doesn't it? Explain to me then please how someone who lost a leg still feels that phantom limb? It's because of the meridian system which holds the energetic pattern within and around the body of the presence of the missing leg. Have you ever had a vibe off someone that gives you the willies? These are all examples of the energy within our meridian system influencing our bodies.

Leanne came to me in the clinic reporting that she felt exhausted and didn't feel comfortable in her workplace. She felt bullied by a manager and felt disrespected because he was taking credit for her work to get promoted. She felt worthless and completely unappreciated. After some initial stress-defusion using zip-up, tuning-in and turning-on techniques I identified stress in her base and heart chakras and her central vessel meridian (see suggested actions below).

Our base chakra is our safe connection to our physical world. There was stress on the affirmation 'I release all negative feelings that hold me back from being happy and free'. There was also spiritual stress associated with actions to satisfy personal needs. On an emotional level, Leanne did not feel secure in her role and her normal calm and confident emotional demeanour seemed to have been flushed down the toilet.

The physiological symptom of an imbalance is associated with our willingness to live and quantity of physical energy. Leanne felt defensive at work, expending her physical energy trying to get everything right and taking on even more work for an incompetent manager. She reported lower back discomfort and on bad days there was pain. There was also significant hormonal interruption from excess cortisol (stress hormone) generating overproduction of aldosterone causing water retention, an overproduction of cortisol contributing to mood swings and fluid retention, and an overproduction of epinephrine causing anxiety and insomnia.

I first balanced Leanne to the energy disturbances I had detected. Everything appeared fine. To challenge that someone's energy systems are balanced thoroughly, I often get them up and off the treatment table to take a quick walk around. I may have them think about the location, person, or event that is their stress trigger.

On this occasion, I guided Leanne into a quick meditation that allowed her to visualise her workspace in a new and safe way. Leanne could then observe her manager and get curious about his behaviour. I instructed her to form a bubble around herself and fill it with golden light. I watched her body soften as she relaxed and embraced the visualisation of golden light.

At the end of that session, Leanne's feedback to me was she saw her manager in a whole new way – now as an insecure person. We practised some coaching techniques and performed a second meditation visualising the workplace.

This time I guided Leanne to view herself as equal to everyone around her, as a confident woman who could calmly communicate her needs and install boundaries that enabled a balanced workload. I also infused the coaching questions into the meditation so she could practise the statement and connect with how this made her feel courageous.

The impact of trauma to your meridian system isn't necessarily from an assault or vehicle accident. It can be as simple as living a busy life and struggling to say no when your work ethic drives you to perform well. When your trauma response has activated a survival switch, your energetic boundaries (that look like confidence and the ability to say 'no') fade. The energetic information exchange between you and your external environment can get confused, interfering with your ability to operate at full capacity. In the example above, Leanne's workplace situation placed stress on her human need for security and this instigated her trauma tale.

> -🔆- **Mountain lion tamer tips to get your energy flowing**
>
> Tune in. The ears contain an entire, miniature version of the body's meridian system!
>
> 1. Check your range of motion of your neck by slowly rotating side to side, you can also twist and bend from your hips. Notice any discomfort or tension.
>
> 2. Rub firmly and slightly tug on earlobes away from your head. This should feel warm and relaxing, any pain and you're being too rough!
>
> 3. Work your way around the entire ear.
>
> 4. Recheck your range of motion to see if the tension has shifted and range of motion improved.

The Schumann Resonance – the planet has a heartbeat

NASA describes the Schumann Resonance as an *atmospheric heartbeat*. Approximately 2,000 thunderstorms are active around the earth at any one time, which produce roughly 50 flashes of lightning every second. Each lightning burst creates electromagnetic waves, which encompass the earth and are captured between earth's surface and a boundary about 30 miles up. Some of these waves – if they have just the right wavelength

– combine, increase in strength and create a repeating, atmospheric heartbeat known as Schumann resonance. Joe Dispenza states that 'the Earth's electromagnetic field has been protecting all living things with this natural frequency pulsation of 7.83 Hz – you can think of this as the Earth's heartbeat'.

Since we are cellular human beings living on a cellular planet, any fluctuation in the frequency of the planet's electromagnetic wavelength or the shift of tectonic plates within the planet influences you from an energetic perspective. There can be a direct influence on your brain waves and your neurological systems within your entire body. This can cause symptoms of tension or anxiety. When you're running a survival program you can experience symptoms of extreme fatigue, disturbances in your sleep, and even clarity of your thinking.

Holy holograms

Peter H Fraser, acupuncture professor, homeopath, TCM practitioner, co-founder of NES Health and author of *Energy and information in nature*, explains how substances and matter have an energetic imprint called the Quantum Electromagnetic Body Field, hereon referred to as the human body field. My head nearly exploded researching this section until I realised that bioenergetics is the study of energy. How does energy translate into our physical, mental, and emotional reality?

ENERGY OPERATES AS A FIELD AND THESE FIELDS CONTROL ENERGY WITHIN ALL LIVING SYSTEMS. INFORMATION-STRUCTURED FIELDS PROVIDE THE FRAMEWORK FOR OUR ENERGY TO BE EXPRESSED –
PETER FRASER & HARRY MASSEY (NES HEALTH)

These fields can be optimised with the information that drives energy exchange. The most simplistic example I can share is your breath. When our posture is slumped, you don't breathe at capacity and turn on your survival switch. When your brain receives information, you sit up straighter to correct your posture and breathe deeper.

Source energy can be considered as life-force energy that represents energy from the quantum zero-point field. From a body-field perspective, source energy is like a driving force within the body and stored in body cavities. Stores of this source energy become depleted by stress, being indoors too much, poor nutrition, and exposure to toxins, and other factors like radiation from devices such as phones and Fitbits. The fluctuations of Schumann Resonance can also deplete your source energy, which influences the probability that your body may not maintain homeostasis which helps you feel unconditionally safe and calm.

American author and spiritual healer Barbara Ann Brennan outlines the parallels between various physics and introduces the concept of *holograms* in her book *Hands of light*. Traditionally, physics studied particles and their waves or the frequencies created as they travelled through space and time. Holograms were first discovered by Nobel Prize winner Dennis Gabor in 1971, who identified a three-dimensional representation of a whole, which can energetically reconstruct the entire image of the particle. Holgrams therefore expanded the science of physics to incorporate dimensions.

Renowned brain researcher Dr Karl Pribram accumulated evidence that the brain's interpretation of our sensory data (sound, sight, taste, touch, and smell) operates holographically. In other words, each fragment of information contributes to the bigger picture.

Dr Pribram, Brennan, Fraser, Mooney and Krebs all reference holographic models to describe how information is sent to our bodies for optimum expression of life from energy fields that surround your body. These fields act like information layers beyond the body as a matrix and combined are called your *aura*. The layers incorporate the following functions:

Layer 1 (Physical) – is the matrix for body tissue formation and physical body healing.

Layer 2 (Emotions) – is the matrix for emotions about ourselves with healing to achieve unconditional self-love.

Layer 3 (Mental) – is the matrix for your logical mind and healing to create positive mindset and thought processes.

Layer 4 (Astral) – is the matrix which holds the record of all your past experiences and healing to achieve unconditional love for others.

Layer 5 (Template) – is the matrix of divine will with healing to gain a sense of truth and purpose.

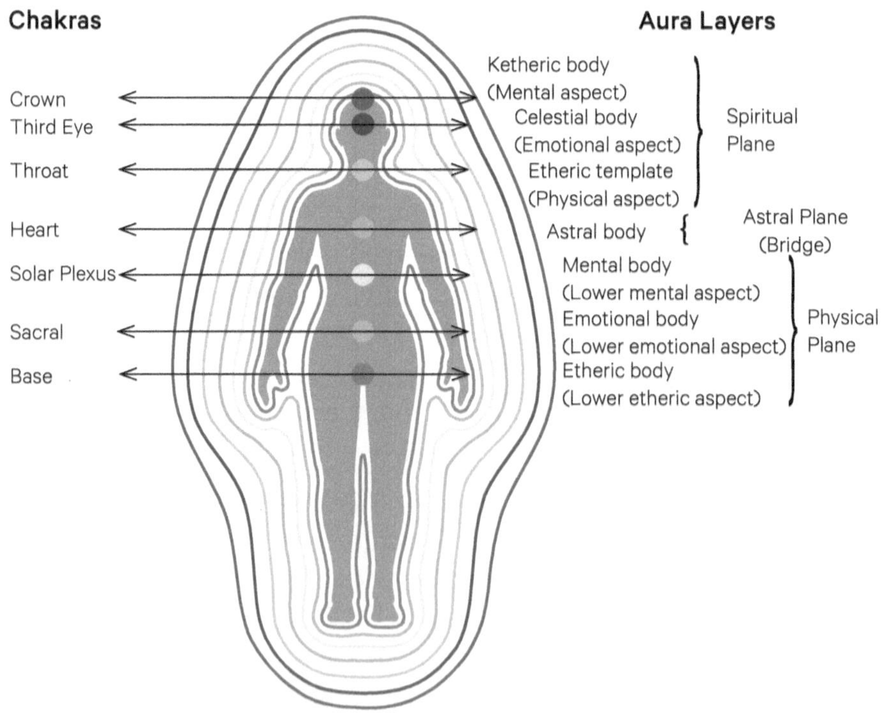

Layer 6 (Celestial) – is the matrix of the divine love and angelic realm, with healing for unconditional love of all creation.

Layer 7 (Etheric) – is the matrix of divine wisdom, with healing to remember the perfection in all life.

At a fundamental understanding, our bodies can regenerate to a point, given the correct circumstances, nutrition, environmental circumstances and access to information within the holographic field. It is well documented in Western science that our physical bodies use RNA to replicate DNA structures for repair and rejuvenation processes, which wear out over time and our bodies commence aging.

Fraser postulated that 'the human body-field requires the presence of gravity and magnetic fields from the planet'. When the transfer of energy, i.e. information, is disturbed, incomplete, non-existent, or distorted like that of a trauma tale or elevated Schumann Resonance, something goes wrong with the body-field's arrangement of energy. Remember we're talking about information to program the body's function. The result is your body responds with a different outcome that isn't optimum health. This is another way to view survival.

Your environment can influence your ability to heal from your trauma tale's raw reaction. Additionally, your trauma tale can distort your human body field via stress in the various energy layers of your aura. The consequences are that your physical body cannot function at its optimum health program. The result is your body adapts to operate a survival program only. The information within your human body field disturbs the expression of information within your biochemical, electrical, neurological, mental, and emotional systems. You can experience these energetic distortions that Western medicine would report as stress symptoms, like anxiety, depression, auto-immune, etc. Therefore, your trauma tale can sometimes feel like life is hard, or you're trapped and can't move forward.

Every particle that comprises a living system in the cosmos has a holographic energy field, which drives the various bioenergetic information to enable you to sustain life. In other words, the energetic information exchange between your hologram or *auric field* and body creates an energetic structure for you to express your best life.

Still with me? Great!

Let me expand the concept of the human body energy field to bioenergetics on a macro scale: the cosmos, the universe, if you will. Just like the planets orbit around each other, we are subtly influenced by these planetary alignments. To make this a little easier to understand, consider the phases of the sun and moon. Picture how you feel when you have had a very late night, partying hard and have to get up super early for an important meeting at work. Do you feel so tired that you are mistaken for being hungover? Can't focus and energy levels are low? Now we are on the same page!

Now picture what your mood is like when it is super windy or bitterly cold? If it does not affect you, ask a schoolteacher; kids and dogs go nuts. Ask a police officer whether they like working full moon shifts; they are going to try to swap to avoid the crazy that oozes out of the societal woodwork.

Just as our environment affects your auric field, so too do substances you ingest, like drugs and alcohol, to name a few. Ask an ambulance officer what the vibe is like from someone who is exceptionally drunk or high. They will tell you there is something a little 'off', or perhaps even toxic.

Now picture that you have activated your raw reaction survival switch and, coincidentally, the weather is humid with a high chance of electrical storms. You are potentially already feeling heightened with no logical known trigger other than the sky is darkening. You can feel sapped of energy by the afternoon storm brewing, even though you slept well.

Your breathing may be affected; there's even electrical storm weather warnings for asthma now! Also, let us look at the classical behaviour of someone experiencing their raw reaction trauma tale; they have a case of can't-be-bothered. It is a very technical term that encompasses mood, motivation and drive.

When you are triggered and feeling low, are you motivated to cook delicious and nutritious meals? – 'Nope.' When you are feeling raw, are you likely to take yourself outside for a walk or sit and watch Netflix? Been there and done that. In all his published work, Fraser discusses that every disease has one common symptom: all have lost energy in the system.

 **Mountain lion tamer tip to clear your holographic field**

1. Limit intake of substances like alcohol or caffeine.

2. Wear or hold rose quartz crystal.

3. Get outside and go for a walk for at least 20 minutes.

4. Put some colour on your plate with a wide variety of seasonal vegetables.

5. Limit exposure to blue light devices.

When you're not yourself

You need to recognise how it feels to experience a moment in time whereby you feel unbalanced and out-of-sorts. Conscious acknowledgement of not feeling great is like arriving at a *choice point* where change is possible. We all have felt that from time to time, right? But imagine feeling not quite right, or not connected to yourself all the time. This is what it can feel like after you've encountered a mountain lion in your fridge. I challenge you to ask yourself how could you possibly heal when you are not yourself and simply reacting to everything that life throws at you?

When you are in the energetic form of *rest and digest*, you can thrive. Yet when you are in the energy of flight or fight, you only have the capacity to survive. When you are in survival mode, your functionality is limited because access to your energetic information is interrupted. You become the tree with destabilised roots that could easily fall over in a strong wind or heavy rain because they simply exist and are not thriving.

People need to connect into themselves first. They need to invest their energy in themselves, focusing on who they are and what they need in that moment to heal and to thrive. To do this, I often find myself coaching clients to detach from the drama of others, as it completely derails their energy systems.

I used the example of when I was entrapped within the mammogram biopsy driver machine. I had split off from myself and dissociated. I was disconnected and completely terrified. This terror caused my voice to become mute. In that moment I felt powerless and unable to advocate for myself and say stop. My mind was scrambled and my energy frenetic from the sensation of wanting to flee and being trapped and that was before surgery or chemotherapy even started. On that occasion I opened the fridge door and the mountain lion reached out with its large sharp claw and scored a point.

Subsequent testing within an MRI machine incorporated confinement with a loud penetrating sound. It is still enough to cause me to split off mid-scan and create massive anxiety moments. During my initial MRI was the time I realised that my trauma response would require significant effort to resolve. I now have many tools and dedicate a lot of planning to prepare for being able to cope during and after this type of trigger.

Clients often feed back that it's confronting to acknowledge their trauma tale. This is because the flight-fight-freeze response has created a sensation of disconnection from self due to the disturbance within your energy hologram. Sometimes the information either cannot be accessed, or you've stored an electrical memory of stress that is being repeated until you heal it. You literally experience emotions of fear, loneliness and disconnection from others, which does not allow you to meet the human need for feeling secure. This can equate to a sense of hopelessness and create distance from you being able to connect with your innate energetic resources of being resilient. The hopelessness robs your physical energy and willingness to act and the downward spiral of illness such as depression or auto-immune disorders begins.

Wrap-up

I have outlined the various energy medicine concepts that incorporate quantum physics and holograms. We are all energetic beings living on a live, energetic planet. We are therefore influenced by everything around us, and what we often do not realise is that we have an incredible amount of energy when stuck in a trauma response, which causes us to overreact to everything around us. In the next chapter, I will personalise the concept of the hologram to support your understanding.

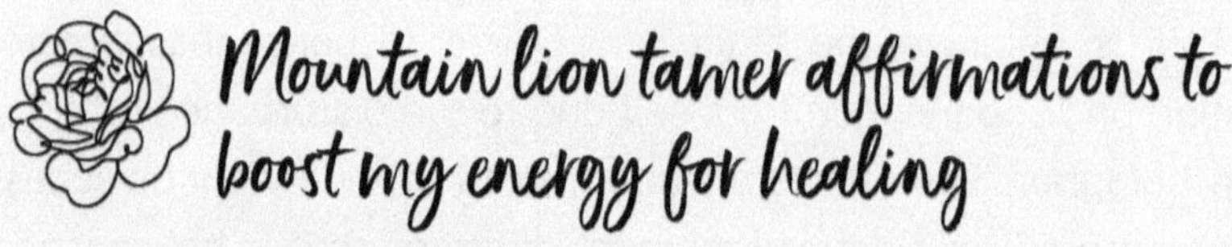# Mountain lion tamer affirmations to boost my energy for healing

Here are some suggested quotes, actions and journal prompts to explore:

Be a DJ and spin your unique soundtrack

1. My spirit is grounded deep in the earth, I am calm, centred, strong and peaceful.

2. I can let go of the fear and trust that I am eternally safe.

3. I am worthy of all things beautiful.

Meridians get flowing

4. I allow my heart to gently open to all possibilities of positivity.

5. I am motivated to seek my true purpose.

6. My energy systems are balanced and work in perfect harmony.

The planet has a heartbeat

7. I listen to my body and its messages of when to *go* and when to *rest*.

8. I allow myself to flow freely with the vibe of the day.

9. I am balanced and grounded, centred and focused.

10. Winter – I surrender to my shadow and its hidden treasure.

11. Spring – I sow the seeds of abundance.

12. Summer – I celebrate my abundance harvest.

13. Autumn – I gather the lessons from my abundance harvest so that I may evolve.

Holy holograms

14. I am connected strongly with my source energy.

15. Accessing my source energy is easy.

16. My auric field is clear and clean.

When you're not yourself

17. Peace is this moment without judgement.

18. You yourself, as much as anybody in the entire universe, deserve your love and affection.

19. I am a conductor of love and light.

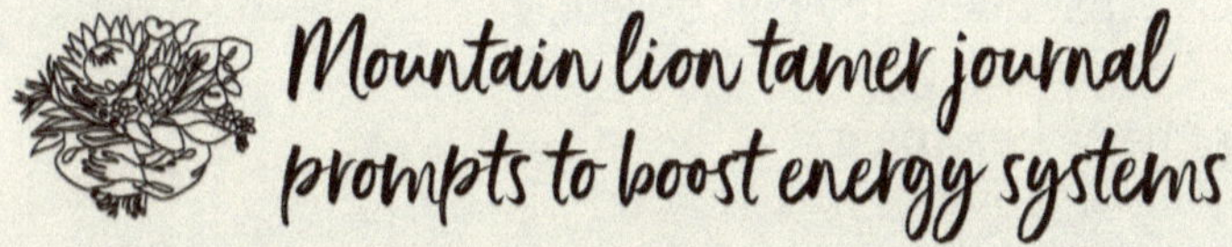

Mountain lion tamer journal prompts to boost energy systems

Be a DJ and spin your unique soundtrack

1. Name a space or place where I feel safe. And list all the reasons why it feels safe on all levels – physical, mental, emotional.

2. How would my life be better if I could gift myself a couple of minutes each day to ensure I am grounded into my life? What might change? What might be the benefits?

Get flowing

3. How are my senses functioning – taste, sight, hearing, touch, smell? How do my senses change over the course of a year? Become aware of how I respond to a particular time of the year – are there any triggers?

4. What are the colours of my wardrobe? Does my wardrobe align with the elemental colours: blue or black (water), green (wood), red (fire), yellow (earth) and white (metal)? Do I tend to wear the same colours throughout the year or am I seasonal by nature? Do I match colours to my mood?

5. What favourite colour do I reach for that invigorates my mood and why?

Holy holograms

6. What do my energy levels say about me today?

7. If I could pause in the midst of busyness, what might I discover in my life that drains my energy levels?

The planet has a heartbeat

8. What might my life feel like if I lived in harmony with everything around me?

9. What might I be attracting into my life right now? Am I focused on more positive or negative?

Chapter Five

Be like a tree, get grounded

The state of grounding ultimately meets your human need for connection. It connects you to the planet you live on, allowing you to feel anchored and secure.

There are many benefits to becoming and remaining grounded. A trauma-based response leaves you with that awful raw reaction after encountering your mountain lion. Let's explore how these energy holograms create a stable foundation for you to become grounded by talking about celestial circuits.

Even though I am a qualified industrial chemist and environmental scientist, it was not until I paired the science with my experiences that I truly understood quantum physics for the gift that it is. I like to understand how everything works and fits together – my inner scientist wants the facts. I nailed my understanding about grounding concepts and how energy works as information when I could feel the experience myself.

Getting grounded is when my inner scientist takes off her lab jacket and my divine feminine jumps for joy. I connect with my innate wisdom.

Was that a pleasurable experience? Absolutely not! Why? Because I did not understand it, and that freaked me out because I felt out of control!

Being grounded is simply a phrase to describe being connected and living your life as the incredible individual that you are. From an energy perspective, it's just like being an old tree with deep roots that dive deep into the earth; your energetic roots ensure you remain in your sacred space to walk your journey path called life.

Imagine how that tree weathers in its environment. Just like in our human life, some days there is sunshine, other days there is wind or a sprinkling of rain. There are days where life feels like a shitstorm and the emotional soil at your feet erodes away, leaving the roots exposed. Have you ever experienced one of those moments?

Ever listened to music and hummed along to the tune? Have you moved your body to the beat and rhythm? This is a very subtle connection to the energetic frequency of sound.

Take this concept another step. Do you feel disconnected or out of sync when you're getting your groove on? Probably not. Grounding is no different, you are simply connecting to the rhythm of the planet. Well, it's the macroscopic or big picture view of grounding.

Emma first came to see me in clinic and then joined my meditation class, intending to heal a deep wound in her heart space. This gap prevented her from ever feeling grounded or centred within herself, which left her always feeling insecure. Emma agreed she was generous in giving out love to others, to the point it left her feeling depleted. During several sessions she came to realise that the energetic exchange with various individuals was never equal. The inequity left Emma perceiving the giving was one way all the time, feeling excluded, waiting for invitation. The consequence was she struggled to receive love.

During her first meditation, Emma visualised entering her heart chakra, later reporting her chest felt warm and golden. With the support of guided intuitive meditation, where I teach everyone how to ground, she realised that unless she could receive love unconditionally, she was blocking her own ability to experience joy and self-love based on an old story.

Emma allowed herself to get curious in the meditation session. She learnt the blockage of receiving love came from the trauma of a primary school bullying incident. Emma's trauma tale left her feeling rejected and excluded. Her curiosity in the meditation revealed she had repeated this trauma tale throughout her life as a pattern.

Emma experienced an epiphany after the meditation when she lived in her heart (rather than in her head where the story was). She grounded in that empowered self-love energy, becoming accountable to herself as an adult. With this new-found awareness and connection to the human need for feeling secure and belonging, she could invite herself back to her heart space. She felt welcomed (human need for belonging) and deserving of receiving the love that she was now free to give herself.

Emma linked this invitation to her heart with being physically grounded. She has now experienced the difference between being ungrounded and feeling internally chaotic, versus being grounded and feeling safe and calm and welcome in her own life. Now with some simple actions she allows the energy of her heart chakra to flow in and out and feel balanced.

Get grounded

Society often refers to people being grounded or centred in terms of their physical and mental state. For example, being confident of oneself, being grounded in themselves. The science of psychology defines being grounded as having a strong connection with who you are, which brings you emotional balance. We are back to the fulfilment of your human needs again.

When I talk about being grounded, I am referring to how you reconnect your physical body to the earth's surface electrons. There is much postulation that *earthing* allows a transfer of negatively charged electrons from the earth's surface into the body. This is a good thing because these electrons neutralise positively charged free radicals within your body that can cause inflammation.

Scientific cancer research suggests that an excess of free radicals within your body damages your cell membranes and DNA, leading to disease. Some research even demonstrates that earthing your body can reduce blood viscosity (thickness) and inflammation. Research has also shown that earthing (grounding) has the potential to support cardiovascular health through calming the tendency to have overactive sympathetic nervous systems (excessive emotional stress). The *Journal of Environmental and Public Health* reports that preliminary studies show 'earthing has a calming and balancing effect on the nervous system'.

Some signs of not being grounded or correctly earthed include:

- Get distracted easily

- Space out

- Overthink or ruminate

- Engage in personal drama

- Experience anxiety and perpetual worrying

- Easily deceived by yourself or others

- Obsessed with your personal image

- Inflammation

- Poor sleep

- Chronic pain.

Are you ticking anything on this list?

Biophysicist James Oschman explains that the moment your foot touches the earth, or you connect to the ground, your physiology changes. An immediate normalisation begins, and an anti-inflammatory switch is turned on. People remain inflamed because they never connect with the earth and the source of free electrons, which can neutralise the free radicals in the body that cause disease and cellular destruction. Earthing is the easiest and most profound lifestyle change anyone can make.

The latest Japanese nature-therapy for stressed-out executives is *Forest Bathing*. After experiencing PTSD myself and the daily benefit from a nature walk and exposure to all that green, which is the colour of the heart chakra, I have firsthand experience of how powerful immersing yourself in nature can be.

Grounding can be as simple as removing your rubber-soled shoes and walking outside in bare feet. It can be a walk in nature to ground you back into your heart space. You can practise purposeful breathing. There is no real limitation in your choice of what works for you. You're only limited if you don't do it!

 Mountain lion tamer tip to get grounded

There are a variety of ways to get grounded:

1. Walk outside in bare feet.

2. Walk in the sand at the beach.

3. Rub the centre of the soles of your feet.

4. Place your feet on the floor, purposefully breathe and bring your focus on parts of your body starting with your head and finishing with your feet.

5. Take a bath with Epsom salts.

6. Use the 5-4-3-2-1 technique – use this when triggered to pay attention to your surroundings. The activity stimulates the senses to enable you to realise you are safe, but also to pay attention to sensory information you would otherwise tune out.

    a. What are five things you can see?

    b. What are four things you can feel?

    c. What are three things you can hear?

    d. What are two things you can smell?

    e. What is one thing you can taste?

Celestial circuit

In my kinesiology training, the *celestial circuit* refers to the inflow of *heavenly chi* or energetic information into your body from the universe. Energy flows through fields and into our holographic form before entering the body. The celestial circuit energy charges up the combination of our meridian system (electrical energetic communication pathways) and our chakras (energy centres for your endocrine program).

In his Life Enhancement Acupressure Protocols (LEAP) training, Dr Charles Krebs states, 'the celestial circuit both receives energetic input from the universe and then transmits this to the person. At the same time, energies of the physical world impact upon the person's electromagnetic structure and function altering patterns of energetic flow.'

Krebs explains that even small fluctuations and minor shifts of electric energetic rises, perhaps those even as small as the early biological patterns of the ovum, can drive the direction of the body's energy into functional configurations. External fields such as man-made fields of electromagnetic devices like 5G towers, mobile phones or microwaves and the earth's geomagnetic field can influence the flow of energy within your celestial circuit. The geomagnetic fields are naturally occurring within the earth. When disturbed, these fields generate *geopathic stress*.

The stability of your neurological function needs to be grounded energetically via your celestial circuit. The quality of energy flowing throughout the celestial circuit therefore has a direct influence on your ability to remain in a state of rest and digest rather than in a state of stress.

Trauma response and grounding

A person can psychologically split off or disconnect during a traumatic experience. This shuts down access to your celestial circuit energy. The science of psychology defines this splitting off as *dissociation,* and it's where a person literally disconnects from the energetic pathway, which drives their physical, mental and emotional ability to cope with life, using their internal resources. The resultant behaviour is a raw reactive state driven by defensive walls, called survival switching.

A trauma response shifts us out of being connected to the earth, being grounded, having energy flow through our body, or having a balanced celestial circuit. Our energy becomes reactive and chaotic. This may explain why some people appear constantly erratic, disorganised or dysfunctional.

If you utilise the science of psychology, your new knowledge of energy systems and the neuroenergetic circuits of the brain, you will understand how an encounter with a mountain lion can drive a trauma response. You can also recognise how a trauma tale can perpetuate when stress in our energy systems is unresolved. Remember the energetic fields and layers around your body have various functions? Let me now explain how your trauma tale influences your energy layers.

The energy of our celestial circuit represents our highest self, versus the ego-self.

Let me use the following statements to demonstrate what I mean.

When there is conflict between your *higher-* and *ego-self*, the stress affects your self-confidence, self-esteem, or even your ability to self-love, and to trust self. Therefore, an encounter with that mountain lion can leave you feeling isolated or alone, needing to feel in control or needing approval from others, with lowered confidence and trust in your ability. Imagine an event so significant that it leaves you feeling isolated for weeks or months on end.

When your survival switch is activated by your trauma tale there are various areas of the brain that are directly influenced by a shift of energy flowing within the celestial circuit. When the brain stem survival circuits have been activated, the survival emotions override access to your higher-self emotions. For example:

- Fear versus love / trust
- Anger versus compassion

- Fight versus surrender

- Flight versus presence.

When you encounter the mountain lion, your reptilian brain activates the survival emotions, which are fear-based behaviours of the flight-fight-freeze response. Imagine living with your life partner whom you love dearly but constantly feel inexplicable anger or rage towards? Frustrating, right?

The *limbic system* in the brain drives our emotional response. When this gets activated, the survival response is to protect your ego first. The limbic emotions which are generated are to reinforce socially acceptable behaviour. For example:

- Reward versus punishment

- Pleasure versus pain

- Good versus bad

- Acceptable and appropriate versus shame blame and guilt.

Your emotional limbic brain deactivates with a trauma tale, leaving you feeling stuck in negative thoughts, feelings and attitudes. Imagine having stress on the pleasure-reward axis? Instead of feeling good when you achieve, your brain automatically switches you to negative feelings of failure and not being good enough.

Our brains' frontal lobes enable us to anticipate future outcomes that are best for us. These are types of positive processing representing the *Yin* and *Yang* of the mind or the rational and the intuitive. For example:

- Discretion versus courage

- Reason versus intuition

- Analysis versus knowing

- Understanding versus comprehension

- Trust versus faith

When you encounter the mountain lion, your frontal lobes can't correctly solution-orientate and therefore your capacity to respond diminishes. This impacts your ability to reason and be rational and therefore becomes the seat of that irrational, raw, reactive-based behaviour. You may experience this when lying down in bed and having a panic attack.

Just like love, energy
is everywhere.

We don't see it, but we feel it. Get out of your head and connect consciously with your heart space. There are endless religious connotations that the heart is the seat of love, emotions and like-minded actions. In modern culture, the heart is referred to in many texts as the locus of our feeling-wisdom, as opposed to our mental-head reason. This definition formulates the basis of what our society refers to as spirituality. Therefore, energetic space of the heart is that magical place where your innate wisdom from the universe is accessed. It's where you send out and receive love. We access the energy of love when our celestial circuit (as defined in chapter four) is free from stress. You feel love when you are grounded.

In clinic, I start all sessions checking the stability of every client's celestial circuit. This is because the celestial circuit is the energetic foundation that stabilises your physical systems. Energy flowing throughout the celestial circuit integrates information within your physical body (via neurons) between your cranial brain, heart brain and gut brain. And I refer to these three areas of the body as brains because of the sheer volume of neuron cells and neural networks. I balance these areas first so that when we migrate into your trauma response, your energy is stable, which enables you to be open to change.

Because we live in a modern, hectic world, your physiological energy struggles to align with the vibration of the planet. Our technology has evolved too quickly; neither our neurology nor our energy systems have adapted to the speed of modern life. Therefore, your neurology perceives many things like microwaves and mobile phones and even Fitbits as an energetic threat. This can cause your body to turn on your survival switch and places stress on your celestial circuit's performance and stability.

Being grounded should feel as if you've returned from a fantastic holiday well rested. It should look like your face and body are calm and relaxed, with your body moving fluidly! I frequently get asked how to do this. So right now, let's get grounded together. But why is understanding what grounding is so important on several levels?

When I first saw little Hudson in the clinic, he was an agitated and frightened little man. His birth had been very traumatic with his mother actively labouring for two days, only to experience a haemorrhage. Hudson was born during the worst case of potential emergency scenarios.

The first thing I noticed was the overly strong attachment to his mother. He never felt safe unless he could touch her. The poor mother was exhausted from constantly reassuring this child he was okay.

I can remember the whole family watching me (they all came to visit the crazy lady with pink crystals on her front porch) as I sat on the floor in front of him and began quietly talking. I explained I was going to use the muscles in his arms and legs to talk to his brain. He wouldn't have a bar of my attempts to placate him. He watched me show muscle monitoring on his father, his siblings and then his mother.

I noticed he was wearing a *Star Wars* t-shirt and asked the family whether they were fans of the series of movies. The animated discussion begun of how one uses the force to make your sister's nose bleed. There was a lot of laughter.

Being cheeky and recognising I needed to engage this kid on his level, I asked him, 'Do you want to learn how to use the force?' This kid's eyes nearly bulged out of his head with excitement.

I used muscle monitoring to show Hudson where his celestial circuit was meant to be anchored at his navel. Hudson's circuit showed he was energetically floating approximately six feet above his body.

The client history form highlighted that Hudson had clinically died at birth and had been resuscitated. Spirit nudged me to ask the parents whether the birth had been filled with excitement. Both immediately tried to hide their tears from the other kids in the room. Clearly the parents had not shared the traumatic birth experience details with their other children. To divert everyone's attention, I asked Hudson whether he ever felt like he was in his body.

He shook his head and replied, 'I never feel like I can get into it. I always feel like I'm floating up here.' I asked Hudson whether he thought he might be afraid all the time because he wasn't in his body. He agreed. Kids really have the most incredible insight and wisdom when you engage with them.

I asked Hudson whether he would like me to use the force and get him back into his body. Needless to say, I threw in a bit of humour, not tickling because that is inappropriate. I used a variety of kinesiology techniques and balanced Hudson's celestial circuit and the trauma he held in relation to his birth experience.

I finished the session inviting the entire family to take part in a guided intuitive meditation whereby everyone focused on the night Hudson was born. This way everyone would get what they needed to heal their own respective trauma. Hudson told me he was no longer floating, and I encouraged him that if he was in his body, he would feel the force every time he got hugged. I reminded him it was now safe to remain in his body. I guided him to focus on his family, who were waiting to give him big, excited hugs. There were many tears of joy as the family embraced after that session.

A couple of days later, Hudson's mother reported her anxious child had disappeared and a confident young boy had emerged. We joked about always using humour and the force to reframe our trauma tale!

It all sounds a little 'woo woo' until you experience and feel the impact of shock and trauma yourself. It's not until you encounter your own mountain lion that you have the experience to recognise the symptoms of the subsequent energetic disturbance within yourself.

It's utterly distressing feeling disconnected from who you are when you're not in your body. You're often left feeling bereft and physically drained. This type of shock can leave you feeling heightened or panicked for hours and days, even months instead of just minutes. Perhaps after reading my stories something may spark within you that your experience may contain whispers of mountain lion encounters as well?

Normally, the body can dispose of the surge of adrenaline in 90 minutes after the shock, however if the trauma is significant and pushes you out of the centre of your celestial circuit, you may in fact struggle to reconnect with your true core of remaining grounded. This makes healing from your trauma tale extremely challenging.

 Mountain lion tamer tips to soothe your system

Grounding exercises are useful to strengthen your tether back to feeling secure within yourself. Link these relaxation techniques with breathing and you're on your way.

1. Take seven drops of Australian Bush Flower Essence Emergency Blend or 'Rescue Remedy' from the English Bach Flower range when in the peak of distress.

2. Rub your Emotional Stress Release points – as per chapter two, page 44.

3. Try an adult colouring book – holding the pencil and touching the paper are both very physical things to do which is useful if you can't get outside to ground yourself.

4. Try a short, guided meditation for relaxation at least once a day – participating in guided meditation takes the pressure off having to create this scenario yourself and you get to surrender a little into the process without there being strength involved.

In my clinical practice, people often try something once (usually on their own without support or supervision) and don't achieve the outcome they desire. The result is they often give up too easily. I constantly link this response back to *shenpa* – we give up too easily when life gets uncomfortable. I coach my clients in consistency and persistence, which is required here to create a body memory of how good it feels to be grounded and have their energy systems balanced.

When you can't restore balance within

The celestial circuit attracts and disseminates heavenly chi into and around the body. It's like taking a bath in universal love. The chi leaves the body via your breath and flows back to the universe. If you were to draw this diagrammatically, it looks like the *Yin-Yang* symbol when one series of energetic information flows and fuels another, and the cycle is endless. If the celestial circuit is not centred, it does not function equally, therefore making us feel off kilter.

Your trauma tale drives a stress response of flight-fight-freeze. What you are often not consciously recognising is that the stress on the celestial circuit drives the emotion of fear, such as fear of being out of control, fear of the future, fear of uncertainty. The list of potential fears is endless. When it comes to fears, this all adds up to a sense of a feeling of helplessness. These unresolved feelings of fear can create a sense of panic. When fear and panic combine, you are left with the resultant physical feeling of being overwhelmed or anxious.

Marianne came to me in clinic one day – she was crying hysterically. A young man trusted by the family had drugged and raped her daughter in their family home. Marianne carried enormous guilt and shame for not being able to keep her daughter safe. She told me she felt utterly exhausted, yet unable to sleep.

Understandably Marianne was extremely angry at this young man, for she had instilled a deep trust in this person to be her daughter's friend and keep her safe. A myriad of negative feelings which caused her to feel completely out of control paralysed her. It was these feelings that were triggering a massive panic attack that was so violent that she would vomit. Nothing of her previously proven relaxation techniques were supporting her.

I balanced her celestial circuit and she was once again able to connect with her logical reasoning skills. Now that she was stable, I could coach Marianne to process this traumatic event so that she could settle herself. She left feeling calm and able to think rationally, feeling empowered with her next steps of what to do to keep her daughters safe.

Wrap-up

I've outlined the various energy systems that drive your ability to function and remain grounded in life, as well as respond to traumatic events. We are all energetic beings living on a live energetic planet. Everything influences us. What you rarely realise is that you use an incredible amount of energy when stuck in a trauma response. This causes you to overreact to everything around you.

Given that modern people don't live in caves like our ancestors, humans aren't able to escape the man-made energy of technology. You need to achieve balance of what energies your body is exposed to in order to achieve an internal calm. Therefore, grounding your body complements your natural state of calm and rest.

So far we've looked at both Western and Eastern philosophies and methodologies, which impact your trauma response, and how this can make you a little bonkers! Bonkers is that feeling of escalated frustration that turns into anger and makes you want to kill someone. Deep down, you know you're not ready to go to prison to act on all those feelings, but what do you do with them?

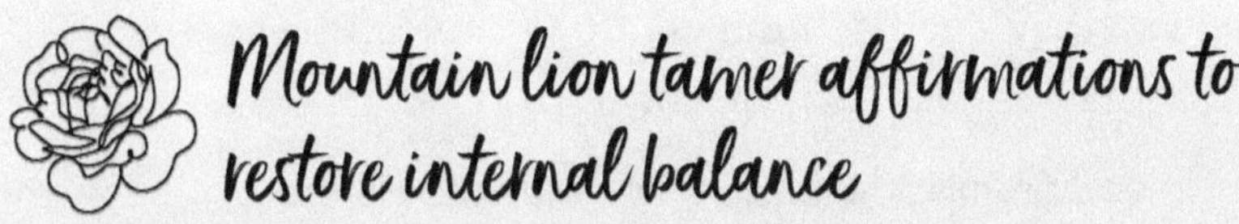 *Mountain lion tamer affirmations to restore internal balance*

Get grounded

1. It is my intention to be grounded, centred, focused, balanced and protected.

2. Spirit keeps me safe wherever I go.

Celestial circuit

3. Peace is this moment without judgement.

4. You yourself, as much as anybody in the entire universe, deserve your love and affection.

Trauma response and grounding

5. I joyously flow with life.

6. I allow myself to step into my rightful space of the universe.

Get grounded activity

This is an activity that you can gift yourself at any time and any place. I often take clinic clients through this process and make a recording so that they can replicate the process at home. I often visualise myself as a tree in a green pasture. Here are some steps you can follow to ground yourself:

1. I focus my attention on my feet, picturing the tree roots exiting out of my feet and into the dirt below.

2. I picture my tree roots flowing down towards the core of the earth through the dirt, through a layer of clay and then rock

until they approach the centre of the earth whereby a red crystal resides. It is Gaia, the earth mother.

3. I seek permission to connect with the centre of the earth. Wrap your tree roots around the red core, sending love to the earth mother Gaia and receive love in return until your roots turn red.

4. Bring that red energy up through where the roots have contacted the crystal, up through the crystal layer, through the bedrock, through the dirt and up into your feet.

5. Allow the red colour of love to enter your feet and rise to your shins and calves, to your knees and then your hips. Feel the strength of the earth mother supporting you from below.

6. Draw your attention upward now, above your head, still picturing yourself as a tree. Picture your hands reaching up to the sky. Allow yourself to become the tree trunk and leaves touching the golden sun of the spiritual father. Again, seek energetic permission to connect with the bright yellow ball of the spirit father that is the sun.

7. Draw the yellow light from the sun into the tips of the leaves, your fingertips, down the branches into your hands and arms. Continue to draw the yellow light down into the top of your head and neck and chest.

8. Now picture the yellow light coming down into your body as if a hand were hugging you from above.

9. Allow the supporting hands of the spirit father to join hands with the mother supporting you from below.

10. Feel the yellow and the red energies merge into orange and send this orange light down to the centre of the earth back up to the sun, creating a figure 8 or infinity symbol of orange

energy flowing through and around you. This mimics the flow of your celestial circuit.

11. Grounded, centred, focused, balanced, and protected, in alignment with the heart of your earth mother and the arms of your spiritual father.

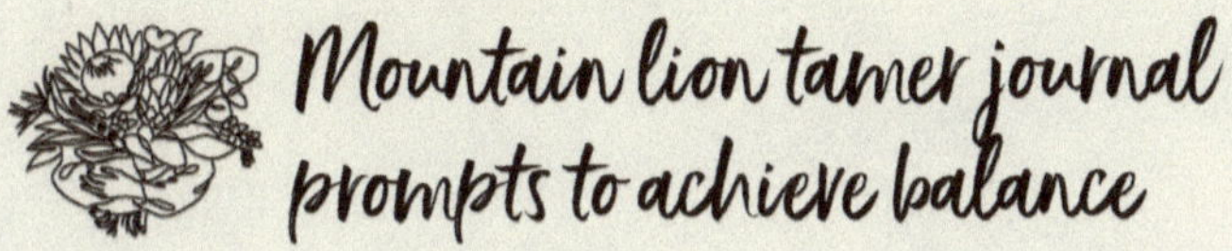

Mountain lion tamer journal prompts to achieve balance

Be a DJ and spin your unique soundtrack

1. Name a space or place where I feel safe. And list all the reasons why it feels safe on all levels – physical, mental, emotional.

2. Would my life be better if I could gift myself a couple of minutes each day to ensure I am grounded into my life? What might change? What might be the benefits?

3. How did I feel before I went for a walk today? And how much better did I feel afterwards?

4. How long a walk did I need to go on to feel that internal calmness?

5. What might happen if I walked outside in bare feet?

When you're not yourself

6. What if I could simply gaze into my own eyes? What makes me uncomfortable about doing this? What do I see? How does it make me feel?

Chapter Six

Sitting with the feels

Your emotions formulate
part of your nature.

One thing I constantly say to clients is whilst we all have thoughts, feelings, and attitudes, they are not designed to squat in the presidential suite of the mind. If ignored and shoved under the metaphorical carpet, you can get tripped up later. This buried stuff can bring you down, or fish-slap you in the face, or just plain push your buttons to make you bonkers. Thoughts and feelings should come and go, rather than getting stuck and forcing you onto the merry-go-round.

Your thoughts, feelings and attitudes form your emotional, energetic state. Function occurs in either of two ways. You can either respond to what happens to you in your life or you can react. Your values and beliefs contribute to your unique way of responding, based on your previous experiences of events being perceived as either good or bad. Your emotional response also depends on whether you are grounded or not, whether your nervous system is running a survival program, and whether your energetic systems are flowing.

Your trauma tale can affect the ability to modulate your mental and emotional responses. There are a bunch of small, actionable solutions to empower you to overcome your own mountain lion encounters, the first being *acknowledgement*.

Feelings is an important topic because it is one of the most powerful tools for healing that I have personally and professionally learnt. Your feelings are the barometer of your state of being. Your mind merely processes your response to life experiences. It is your heart space that is the ruler. Acknowledging how you are feeling can be like using the master key for any door that holds memories of experiences in your mind. Once you acknowledge what it is you are feeling, you can become curious and begin understanding your why.

Please recognise that whilst I'm a multi-disciplinary practitioner, I don't fix you. My role is to create a safe space for you to fix yourself. I support you in understanding your response to your experiences. And I make every attempt to defuse your response to stress so that you may recuperate from your trauma tale.

THERE IS ONLY EVER ONE PERSON WHO CAN FIX YOUR FEELINGS, AND THAT'S YOU!

Let's explore the concept of acknowledgement. The more you allow yourself to understand about what and why you're feeling without judgement, the more you learn how to discern your current response. You can become accountable for your current response by reframing a past tense reaction. Acknowledging how triggers make you feel defuses the built-up emotional energy of the original trauma. Acceptance makes it easier for you to process the triggers that continue to arise. Processing heals your emotional wounds. This is how you transform your own trauma tale.

This transformation requires you to embrace your courage, to overcome the anchored weight that emotional energy brings to your trauma tale. This chapter will explore how you can build confidence to face the uncomfortable feelings you've been stuffing under the carpet and avoiding all this time. I will explain how to feel safe sitting in all those feelings, how you become your own teacher as you embrace your *shenpa*, which triggers the emotions of your first encounter with that mountain lion.

Big girl pants

Western culture does not promote that you are your own healers. The Global Wellness Institute estimates that the global wellness economy in 2020 was worth $4.5 trillion! Our quick-fix, pop-a-pill culture incorporates the avoidance of feelings through the 'fake it till you make it' gloss of social media. In other words, shove your feelings under a rock so that you can fake it and look and act like an airbrushed supermodel living a fabulous life! But you never see that supermodel binge-eating everything in the cupboard and then having a good cry. You rarely see the pictures of sadness, tears or the ugly side of themselves. You see pictures of someone flogging themselves at the gym, but you don't see the day after pictures, when they are so sore they can't wipe their own bottoms.

Currently, society promotes seeking an external validation of your health and wellbeing, through polished marketing of the magical quick fix. What ever happened to measuring your own barometer by asking yourself, 'So how are you today?' In her TedTalk, 'How to stop screwing yourself over', Mel Robbins encourages her audience to ditch the automated response of 'I'm fine' when asked how they are. I share her philosophy and routinely ask clients, 'When will it be time to be truthful with yourself?'

Mel states that, 'We have life-changing ideas for a reason and it's not to torture yourself'. Substitute the word ideas for experiences and the message is still the same. Spirit doesn't dish out trauma for fun, it's so we can learn lessons at a deep level. This is demonstrated by world renowned medical intuitive Caroline Myss, who states in her book, *Anatomy of the spirit: The seven stages of power and healing*, that 'you have to get acceptance to move from the mental into the physical level of your body, to feel your truth viscerally and cellularly'.

My take on this is simple – you need to feel your experience from your heart, as this is the organ that measures your language of how well you live your life. The heart language should include love, joy and gratitude. I would add that you have experiences in your life that gift you lessons to grow and evolve. It's a choice to reframe aspects of your life as periods of lessons being learnt rather than feeling like you're attending a 'shit festival'.

WE ALL HAVE THE POTENTIAL TO BECOME OUR OWN HEALER.

My disclaimer is that you must decide you want to heal. It's that simple. It's the implementation of that decision that is challenging. Act and be the driver of your change process, and this takes effort. Be brave enough to act. Courageous enough to face all that stuff that makes you uncomfortable. Be brave enough to be consistent and continue taking forward steps to ensure progress, because there are days when you will stumble. And that's okay; those are the days where spirit is nudging you to pay very specific attention to something. There will always be what we initially perceive as obstacles and hurdles.

Using the power of reframe, you can choose to look at these aspects of life as detailed lessons to be learnt as you heal from your trauma response. It's like learning maths. You don't jump into algebra. First you learnt to count. Then you learn times tables, followed by addition and multiplication. The method of learning life lessons is the same principle, it's an evolution of applying knowledge of what brings you joy and repeating that pattern.

Not going to lie, there are days when you will feel intense. These will be the days when you will fully immerse into healing your trauma tale. When I'm in the thick of my feelings, I can feel like I've fallen to the bottom of a hole. It is in this dark that I learn to celebrate. I celebrate because I'm no longer opposing the barriers, challenges, the hurdles or the obstacles. I'm allowing myself to surrender fully to the experience so that I may appreciate how the lesson makes me feel so I can be accountable and, where required, fine-tune my behaviours, thoughts and attitudes. I embraced the gift of my experiences, my *shenpa*.

The Merriam-Webster Dictionary defines courage as 'mental or moral strength, to venture, persevere, and withstand danger, fear, or difficulty.' I would expand this to include that courage gives you the strength to make a commitment to sit in your own stuff, all that emotional baggage you've been avoiding, which makes you uncomfortable. To connect with all those feelings and not freeze or run away metaphorically, i.e. to run that switching survival program, you must first feel safe.

My wish for you is to allow yourself to experience your emotional stuff as a gift too. Let's look at how you can connect with the feelings that you've been hiding. You may also find it useful to identify where your body stores the energy of these buried emotions and how that can leave you feeling drained and stuck. Hopefully, this will enable you to gain clarity on how hanging on to this negative energy impacts your life and stops you from healing from your trauma tale.

Jackie, a marathon runner, first came to see me with a sore ankle. During the session we uncovered that she'd fought with her husband just before she sustained the injury. I asked Jackie whether she had acknowledged her feelings about the argument and whether she had resolved things with her partner.

Normally very reserved, Jackie surrendered into these buried emotions with a huge cathartic crying session. Often when people do this, they get extremely hot as they release trapped emotional energy. The release of emotions allowed Jackie to recognise a pattern of sabotaging close relationships whenever she felt insecure. This pattern triggered enormous judgement of self. I reminded her we were on a journey of discovery for information and she could lay down the pattern of shame, blame and guilt – much like placing down heavy luggage full of concrete.

With some breathing exercises to settle her anxiety, Jackie could calmly acknowledge fears associated with those feelings of insecurity. She realised that her resultant behaviour was to pick fights to feel like she was in control. Up to that point, Jackie realised she avoided exploring this pattern because it generated her symptoms of crippling anxiety, which made her feel extremely uncomfortable and frightened. She left the session feeling empowered that anytime she felt overwhelmed, all she had to do was visualise herself at the airport and check her unwanted luggage in to the 'no longer required flight' and head for a new destination!

I remind my clients to embrace their courage to face their stuff. It's important to remember you don't always need to analyse or understand what it is you are exploring. The awareness often gently arrives once you have calmed and cleared your mind. Other times you don't need to know because you were a silent participant in someone else's lesson.

Sometimes in the heat of anxiety, despair or that suicidal ideology, you simply need to recognise that your shenpa has arisen. That moment you consciously acknowledge something has triggered you is a gift. The gift is the exact moment you get to choose to step out of that stress reaction habit.

Historians will refer to 2020 as the year a global pandemic consumed us. For me, it was the year I summoned all my energy and resources to embrace courage – to process the symptoms associated with Post Traumatic Stress Disorder (PTSD) after my entrapment biopsy experience. Using courage enabled me to take charge of my healing process. Courage was like my big girl pants. Courage helped me stop wallowing in self-pity and pick myself up off the floor. Again, and again and again. Healing involves putting on your metaphorical wonder woman knickers and taking action.

Let me be very clear. Taking charge of your healing process and being courageous does not stop the symptoms of your trauma tale. Being courageous empowers you to become accountable – to yourself. Remaining conscious enables you to realise when you're running your trauma response pattern(s). Being courageous is a gift to yourself which supports you in those moments of crisis. Courage gifts you the moments to take that purposeful breath and step out of reaction and back into the space of response.

Brené Brown defines courage as 'a heart word', which has evolved to what you can associate with being heroic, brave, or speaking your truth. Just like Mel Robbins's message, Brown recognises there is also inner strength and a level of commitment required for you to speak honestly and openly about who you are and about your experiences – good and bad. Therefore, speaking your truth is acknowledging what feeling is arising.

Imagine if you could take Robbins's and Brown's definition a little further and become your own superhero just by acknowledging what you feel and speaking your truth from your heart space. Now imagine you could feel courageous enough to speak to your reflection in the mirror. Go the whole nine yards and start a conversation with your own inner child. How might life be different?

YOUR INNER CHILD IS THE ENERGETIC VERSION OF SELF THAT HAD ALL THOSE FIRST EXPERIENCES AND HOLDS THE INFORMATION ASSOCIATED WITH YOUR JOY AND TRAUMA.

Sounds a little far-fetched, doesn't it? What I mean by this is that one of the key steps to heal your trauma tale is to recognise your shenpa. This means acknowledging the feelings that arise within you, acknowledging what is deep inside you, sitting quietly, and allowing yourself to become curious about when those feelings first started. Gaining this knowledge grants you infinite wisdom about why you behave or react in a certain way.

When you deny yourself the experience of feeling and expressing out those negative emotions, it creates emotional and mental energetic blockages. These blockages affect your meridian and chakra energy systems and can even affect the flow of energy within your celestial circuit. Therefore, when you're entrenched in a trauma response, you may not believe consciously that you are capable, or worse, worthy of change. This equates to self-doubt.

I regularly see self-doubt expressed in my clinical space. Clients object or doubt the use of courage and that becoming their own superhero is neither possible nor necessary. What I explain to clients is that facing self-doubt gives you the ability to gain an understanding of that rawest, most vulnerable part of yourself.

> '**I KNOW YOU ARE HURTING—REALLY BAD. I WILL NOT TELL YOU TO LOVE YOURSELF OR SMILE, BUT TO KEEP SURVIVING, TO GET THROUGH THIS DAY, TO EAT WHATEVER YOU WANT AND NOT FEEL GUILT. I WILL NOT TELL YOU TO STAY IN BED FOR A WEEK, A MONTH OR A YEAR IF THAT IS WHAT YOUR SOUL NEEDS. I WILL REMIND YOU THAT YOU ARE STILL BEAUTIFUL, EVEN WHEN YOU ARE DRESSED IN ALL THE GRIEF.'**

RUNE LAZULI

This feeling of self-doubt (which conventional medicine clinically diagnoses as generalised anxiety disorder) is like noisy monkey chatter – the incessant internal dialogue that does laps inside your head. Self-doubt can include exaggerated negative or irrational thoughts. The voice inside your head that vomits up statements like 'you're not good enough', 'you're wrong', or 'it's not worth speaking up or taking action' can be quite noisy and even convincing. Often this voice is full of crap.

The energetic expression associated with when you avoid or ignore your reactive emotions, thoughts, attitudes and behaviours can feel bonkers. It's the shenpa itch. The broiling energy within you when triggered can make you feel you want to scream the roof right off the house. The day of my breast biopsy made me feel like that.

After my biopsy experience, for months I experienced flashback episodes. Each left me feel extremely angry, heightened, and not safe, even in my home. This was a terrible blow to someone who spent the last twenty years working on herself to feel empowered, strong, and worthy about herself.

Within that hour and a half of being trapped in that machine, I felt like I had lost everything I had ever worked for. The biggest loss was the shock robbing me of my ability to speak up during the testing and feeling bullied into having a second biopsy when I already wasn't coping with the situation.

I recall the radiologist telling me that the surgeon needed two biopsies. My flashbacks include vivid recall of my thoughts 'Tell him no! Tell him to stop.' I heard screaming inside my head and felt my body switch on full alert since I could not move. Even despite being pinned down by the machine, my voice would not work. My eyelids did not work. I was aware of blood from the first biopsy dripping down my arm. I could hear the droplets hitting the floor, which the nurse slipped in. Despite that, I could not speak up. I could not even open my mouth, and the screaming inside my head continued.

My survival program had kicked in, and I wasn't fleeing or fighting. I had completely frozen, especially my voice. Yet I felt all the feelings, all at once, with no way to express them.

My therapists have supported me to work through the entrapment experience with countless hours of crying. I still have issues lying on that left side with my arm over my head and still cry in that position, especially as the massage therapist works on my shoulder girdle. I process those tears now as a gift. The tears support me to release that emotional energy still entrapped within the soft tissue.

When Kylie first massaged me after the surgery, I burst into cathartic tears. She paused, thinking I was in pain. Finally, I could speak about what I was feeling. I now see this as a gift for her too. Let me explain.

Kylie, like so many others in my extended tribe of sisterhood, desperately wanted to do something for me after my diagnosis and surgery. Kylie gave me a safe place to reprogram my body so I could lie again on my left side and feel safe. During that massage, Kylie replicated the position that I was in in the mammogram machine. She massaged the tension out of my body and gave me the space and the safety to connect with my voice. That primal voice that I released during that first session moved us both, and it's something that will stick with me for the rest of my days.

Kylie and I speak of this moment often, about how therapists stand in the space of clients' emotions and their mental energy, otherwise known as their auric field. As therapists, it exposes us vicariously to your trauma energy when we work on you.

Nowadays, whenever Kylie works on that specific spot of my body, I am proactive and always ensure that we are laughing first. I am purposefully and consciously replacing any negativity and trauma in my physical soft tissues with joy and love, absorbing Kylie's kindness with every stroke. If that's not a gift, I don't know what is.

I guess making this point gives me the opportunity to remind you, when you're not in survival mode as you work through your emotional trauma response, you receive gifts. Importantly, you get this beautiful opportunity to reflect on situations and events and see them for what they are. Remove the judgement and you are left with just experiences.

EXPERIENCES ARE GIFTS OR OPPORTUNITIES TO LEARN ABOUT YOURSELF AND SOMETIMES WHEN YOU'RE ABLE TO SIT BACK, YOU REALISE THAT AS SHITTY AS AN EXPERIENCE CAN BE, THE FLOW-ON EFFECT OF WHAT YOU LEARN ABOUT YOURSELF IS INCREDIBLE. THIS IS OFTEN WHY PEOPLE AROUND YOU MAY HAVE TROUBLE BEING COMPASSIONATE ABOUT YOUR SITUATION. THEY HAVE NO PERSONAL REFERENCE TO YOUR SITUATION, SO THE STRESS IS UNIMAGINABLE.

It's the perfect opportunity perhaps for you to think about how you can reframe from maintaining a flight-fight behavioural pattern and learn how to embrace situations and your emotional response to them. Embracing the emotions creates energy to become willing to get curious about your why.

Consider the energy expenditure from holding on to the emotional negativity of the trauma response; you can then understand the effort required to keep these emotions within yourself. It really takes superhero qualities to lift the lid on the treasure chest of where you've stuffed it all inside and slowly let it all out.

There are exceptions to this point of embracing courage. Whilst the peace-love-mung beans approach to loving self sounds awesome, it requires you to take action and often as baby steps. You can feel extremely raw and vulnerable when sitting in all those trauma emotions.

You might like to start simply with journalling the feelings associated with being triggered. If that is too much, a simple walk outdoors is a lovely and gentle kickstart to soothing an emotionally frazzled system. Still no relief? Try pounding a pillow, especially if angry. This isn't a ticket to take a pillow to work and smash someone's face. This is a safe technique for you to release intense built-up anger. Sit on your bed and allow yourself to think of what made you mad. Allow the anger to rise until you've no choice but to take hold of a pillow, raise it above your head and pound it downwards onto the bed. A small chair cushion is perfect for this.

Start this process slowly, with small implementable actions. Otherwise, you risk feeling extremely heightened and raw. I highly recommend seeking professional help to kickstart your progress if you feel unsafe, or uncertain how to do it on your own. Do whatever aligns to your belief system and by that I mean it might be a psychologist or a counsellor or even a kinesiology practitioner that you engage. You might prefer a meditation or yoga to get you into a space where you feel safe and comfortable within yourself to find the courage to get curious enough to explore deeply within. You might even like to commence with a quick brisk walk, as movement supports your body to release unwanted negative emotion.

 **Mountain lion tamer tips to embrace your courage and big girl pants**

1. Pound the pillow when the emotional energy rises.

2. Do something that makes you sweaty (like a brisk walk) and can safely unleash your negativity.

3. Write about a trigger event or name and place it in your shoe and stomp out your frustration.

4. Scream out the feelings from the mountain top, shower or into a pillow.

5. Allow yourself to have a great big cry (again, shower is brilliant for this).

6. Journal out the feelings with a side of curiosity:

    a. Start with dot points of everything you're feeling.

    b. Write a 'fuck you' letter.

    c. Write about the trigger event.

    d. Allow yourself to take stock of how you feel after everything is out of you and on paper.

Remember Pema Chodron's words about our *shenpa*? We train ourselves from an early age to avoid uncomfortable. Sitting in your feelings takes commitment and dedication to healing. It takes practice to unwind a knot that has been tied forever. Go watch Mel Robbins's TedTalk. Our emotions, such as discomfort, are a signal that somewhere in your life your human needs are not being met rather than as a source of self-torture.

Is today the day you'll stop ignoring that discomfort and allow yourself to get curious?

Have a little faith

Edith Eger is the critically acclaimed author of *The gift: 12 lessons to save your life*. She shares her story of surviving the Holocaust and another of kidnapped children escaping from where they had been hidden because they had a little faith in themselves whilst some remained paralysed and stuck by their captor. When you activate your courage, your energy expands to allow you to become curious. This curiosity allows you to explore what you've metaphorically shoved under the carpet and avoided. Curiosity gifts you permission to acknowledge those parts of you that have been hidden so you can embrace the lesson to be learnt and get on with your life. It's like putting a fresh set of batteries in your torch so that you can finally shine a light in a dark room.

Acknowledging what you discover when you get curious is confronting. Bessel van der Kolk, world renowned trauma expert and author of *The body keeps the score*, states, 'it takes enormous trust and courage to allow yourself to remember.' When stuck in your trauma tale, you can experience shame when remembering an event: the negative evaluation of self with associated feelings of distress for your actions or even inaction. The shame arises because your survival switch activates. The emotional response from the original trauma is reactivated. Van der Kolk states, 'traumatised people tend to superimpose their trauma on everything around them and have trouble deciphering whatever is going on around them.'

The survival switch inserts the wrong filter for emotional or mental interpretation of what is happening right now. For example, when I didn't feel emotionally numb, I felt a horrendous shame after my biopsy experience. I inappropriately questioned my validity as a practitioner since I was suffering from PTSD. Shame is like putting on a tight jumper that reduces our ability to move our arms or turn our head from side to side. Shame, blame, guilt drive punishment and avoidance patterns which are counterproductive to curiosity.

Dr van der Kolk clarifies this by stating that 'trauma reorganises how your brain manages practitioner-exceptions, changing the way you think, act and reduces your capacity to think. For real change to take place, the body needs to learn that the danger from the trauma event has passed and you are now safe to live in the reality of the present.'

When you connect with your purpose of your life, your faith in self becomes an incredible motivator that supports curiosity. It can begin with a simple question, made famous by Dr Phil: 'How's that working for you?' The power of this single question, even mimicking the good doctor's voice, is harnessing the positive power of reframe.

When you can reframe, you are pausing the energetic emotional connection to negativity and stepping out of the emotional state to examine what is occurring. The action of reframing supports you to use your emotional energy to dial down your neurological survival switch. As soon as the logical frontal cortex can be engaged, the brain realises you aren't under threat. It is at this point that your courage and curiosity support you to realise you are in fact safe, and you are capable of change.

I always recommend starting small, for example, with focused *in-the-moment* actions like using afformations. When it comes to your trauma tale, and when your logic brain is detached due to the survival switch, affirmations aren't enough. Afformations, on the other hand, are fabulous. Afformations are the abundance (in terms of awareness) you catch using your shenpa hook! Let me explain. When you are triggered, and the former unresolved emotional energy arises, you feel the discomfort in your body. You are reacting. The afformation enables you to ask a logical question, 'What might my life be like without these feelings?'

In the peak of my PTSD period, I struggled to do the most basic of tasks. It didn't help matters that I was having chemotherapy treatment at the same time. I attempted meal planning and couldn't for the life of me remember the recipes, let alone the ingredients. My teenage daughter had to get cookbooks out and help me make the shopping lists. This gave me incredible anxiety that caused me to panic because I could not remember the simplest of things. The consequence was that even the simplest of conversations were exhausting and panic filled.

I enrolled in an intuitive meditation course hoping that I'd learn some new skills (or resurrect some old ones) to help me relax and not overreact to my family. Learning about breath soothed my nervous system. I reminded myself that chemo wouldn't be forever, and that it served a purpose. The modules encompassed topics like self-love, letting go, and forgiveness.

It was using this new practice that I reconnected with my breath and allowed myself to sit still and simply acknowledge the panic, 'What might my life be like if I could just lay down the panic?' I recall vividly that I instantly took a deep breath and sighed, my shoulders dropping and the tears rolling down my cheeks. Finally, the feelings dam broke, and I could release a tsunami of emotional turmoil that had been brewing from the entrapment experience.

This release paved the way for the afformation of 'What might my life be like if I could accept my situation right now?' I answered this question with the realisation that I was experiencing a mindset with associated emotions of being a victim. I journalled out all the victim statements and feelings, and I felt lighter. The anxiety faded, and I could immerse myself into the meditation sessions.

I continued to ask myself that question again and again and again. It was like peeling another layer back to expose parts of my emotional web. It gave me permission to seek the solution to accept my situation. That is what afformations do! This is when I started having fun at oncology and made those sessions my bitch! That single question paved the way for me to step out of victimhood and realise chemo would only be for a couple of months. My logical thinking returned. I could surrender to the anxiety and accept that I was having 'down time' and accept the period that I received oncology treatment. My anxiety had been contributed to by the unresolved emotions of the entrapment and my guilt of not working in the clinic.

Caroline Myss states that 'learning the language of the human energy systems is a means of self-understanding'. You use experience of emotions to decode what you can't say. You learn from the expression of experience. Your digestive language breaks down food into biochemical code that works with the oxygenation process from your respiratory system to drive energy manufacturing processes within your cells. The brain carries information into patterns to create waves and record memories of your perceptions of your experiences. Your auric-field is the energetic cell by which you function as a whole to formulate your rightful place in the cosmos.

WE ARE ALL SIMPLY STARS, SOME SHINE BRIGHTER THAN OTHERS.

Levine outlines that you all have survival strategies, which are the behaviours you learnt from a first threat. You convert this to survival knowledge by adapting to your environment quickly and effectively. The second exposure or phase of normalising your trauma response, like animals do in the wild, is to undertake a playful replay. This is demonstrated in nature as aggressive play between animals where they're learning how to defend themselves.

In reality, when you face similar circumstances, you have a huge energy surge to enable you to activate the flight-fight-flee response. That energy then discharges into running scenarios of what if this or that happened. You become completely exhausted after expending your physical energy to do all that analysis and therefore need to rest.

The issue with traumatic events is this: as humans often you don't discharge all the energy used to mobilise yourself from the event. When your brain reviews the information of the trauma event, the person is still maintained in a highly trauma-induced energised state. It's this mental replay of what could have happened and the arising fears (emotional energy) associated with various scenarios that are also incorporated into your memory. Therefore, your brain creates a record of the emotional energetic output to defend you, which is logged into your memory to enable you to respond the same way next time.

It is this fear recording that contributes a significant portion of your trauma response behavioural pattern in a hyper-arrest state. In chapter two, I explored the survival switch being an incomplete response to the threat because the brain has bypassed the extra thinking to find the fastest solution to survive. Therefore, trauma events recorded in your memory systems for later recall are mostly fear-based because you're missing lots of logical information.

The brain stores the instruction of how to interpret and respond to a trauma. You hold the undischarged energy from the actual trauma or replay in your cellular body. This means when you revisit trigger scenarios, your body's energy field experiences the emotions first, followed by the brain, and it impacts both your emotional, and mentally based rational response. This is also how you become reactive from an emotional perspective.

It's vital to remain connected to your faith, that deep belief in yourself. When you lose faith, you lose trust in yourself. When you lose faith in self, the consequence is your self-worth plummets and your ability to 'speak up' and tell your truth is diminished.

Becoming aware

I've lost count of the number of times an adult client sees me and confesses for the first time to experiencing sexual abuse or physical violence from a parent as a child. For these people, this trauma is like a dirty little secret that had burdened them since the incident. Their expected emotional responses of anger, rage, terror and even helplessness are entrapped within the survival switch and often masked as inexplicable pain somewhere in their body. A common behavioural trait they all display is a displacement in their faith of themselves, as well as lack of trust in self and others.

These clients often report experiencing flashbacks or persistent nightmares. Van der Kolk attributes this phenomenon to the brain shutting down Broca's area (speech) with activation of the survival switch, and the visual cortex lighting up. Therefore, your brain preserves only snippets of the perceived image that have associated emotions which aren't resolved, leaving you feeling frightened.

Katie has experienced a strained relationship with her mother her entire lifetime and felt incredibly frustrated, angry and rejected every time we worked on this topic. She first came to me conflicted. She desperately desired to be lovingly nurtured by her mother yet fulfilled the role of mother in the relationship with her parent. I defused the stress associated with this relationship and guided Katie into a heart space meditation.

This exercise provided several gifts. First, she could unpack this unrealistic expectation she had placed on her mother and be kinder to herself from getting frustrated. Secondly, Katie now realised that her mother had not been capable of ever meeting this expectation because her mother won't take responsibility for her stuff, as she was emotionally stuck in her past. With this new perception and understanding, Katie can now choose to accept her mother from a fresh perspective – that her mother is human. Katie now has the capacity to learn how to mother herself whilst sending her mother unconditional love.

This is another reason to have a little faith when you are triggered. Your brain bypasses the time passed since the trauma and simply retrieves trigger memories into real time. It's as if whatever happened a long time ago is happening again, right now. Reminding yourself to have faith allows you to prompt yourself to reframe a negative situation. This step enables you to acknowledge more readily what you are feeling without the trauma being so sharp a stab in the back.

Levine emphasises the need for faith by stating 'without awareness we have no choice'. I am living testament that as you work through your stuck emotions of your trauma response, you can become more self-assured, connected to passion and happiness – you become connected to living instead of surviving.

'Every trauma provides an opportunity for authentic transformation. Trauma amplifies and evokes the expansion and contraction of the psyche, body and soul. It is how we respond to a traumatic event that determines whether trauma will be a cruel and punishing Medusa turning us into stone, or whether it will be a spiritual teacher taking us along a vast and unchartered pathway.'

Peter Levine

In her book, *From crappy to happy*, clinical and coaching psychologist, mindfulness meditation teacher Cassandra Dunn also refers to using your stress hook to defuse stress. Another hook reference! I have reworked Dunn's ideas to create a link to your hooks through the following steps:

1. Give yourself permission to recognise when you are hooked in the trauma response (you'll know this because it's uncomfortable).

2. Gently allow yourself to drop down into your heart space where the feelings reside and the safe place where you can get curious.

3. Catch yourself when your monkey chatter is analysing, nasty or negative, and acknowledge this is simply a sign you are stuck in your head.

4. Allow yourself 'self-soothing' like reframing or using afformations. Dunn, Levine and Chodron all refer to this as detaching from the hook.

5. Give yourself permission to feel all the feels – just don't let them bog you down!

6. Try journalling or meditation to quieten the mind and allow your body to gently release information.

7. Allow yourself to experience the physical sensation of pent-up emotions by thumping a pillow or stomping on the spot.

8. Utilise mindfulness or guided meditation to transform the physical sensation.

There's no rocket science here, folks. Just have a little faith and pick one to try what resonates for you. Having faith in yourself is invigorating. Nurturing ourselves and giving ourselves love is the ultimate gift. Loving others unconditionally, despite their flaws, is simply good karma. Becoming consciously aware of when you are hooked is challenging and confronting, but also a gift in your healing.

The objection I constantly hear in the clinic is 'this is hard'. My response is multifaceted:

1. 'No one likes broccoli, but it's so good for you!'

2. What's the consequence of remaining in this pattern right now?

3. How does holding on to this trauma response pattern serve you?

4. What are you getting from it?

5. Be kind to yourself; you don't heal overnight. You've spent your lifetime getting to right now, so cut yourself some slack!

You need to understand your limits and what you are capable of right now. After all, your body thinks and is reacting as if the trauma is still happening.

 **Mountain lion tamer tips to becoming aware**

1. Identify strategies that make you feel safe when you are triggered.

2. Be honest with yourself and identify your top three trauma response triggers – mine is being lied to.

3. Write a list of potential quick action(s) you can take when triggered:

   a. Post the list on the fridge (this helps you to be accountable because it's public and it empowers loved ones around you to know what to do when you turn into a meerkat).

   b. Use slow, purposeful breath for 60 seconds.

4. Ask for a hug.

5. Instruct a loved one to remind you that you are safe. 

Depending on how severe your symptoms are in responding to trauma, it may be safer for you to work with a qualified therapist. This allows the combination of trained supervision that provides guided structure to ensure you are safe at the beginning of your healing journey. Additionally, a trained professional can identify simple strategies for your specific circumstances.

Sit in your shit

To heal, you must allow yourself to acknowledge what you feel when your trauma response is activated. The challenge is you have to feel safe enough to allow yourself to sit in all the feels. This step is like boosting your faith with a little testosterone and scaling up to believing you are safe. After all, what is the worst that could happen? Will the trauma happen again if you analyse it or might you just feel crappy for a while? The true healing gift is allowing yourself to connect with the emotional feeling, acknowledge it and then allow it to pass. You don't always need to analyse and understand but recognise your *shenpa*. The hook has been activated.

According to Richard Utt, author and founder of applied physiology, attitudes give rise to behaviours. When attitude aligns with thoughts (about the trauma event) an inner conflict is created. Because of the trauma event and internal conflict, intense emotions are generated which cause mental and emotional pain, otherwise known as a reaction.

In his applied physiology training courses, Utt taught that correcting the overlying attitude is only a temporary fix, and that the primary issue to address was the need to address the feelings. In my extensive kinesiology training I learnt that the throwaway advice of 'just get over it' can never work because the negative feelings of the original trauma have been interwoven into your resultant survival program and behaviours.

You can use journalling to purge these feelings. You can also make significant personal discoveries about emotional stress with the use of afformations. The Collins Dictionary defines an affirmation as 'a question that a person asks themselves as a form of self-help through positive thinking'. Affirmations focus on the positive; the difference with afformations, however, is asking a positive question rather than using the statement, which enables you to explore what the subconscious mind is responding to more effectively than simply using the statement as a mantra repeatedly without conscious knowledge of the underlying issue.

I've not met a single person on the planet yet who enjoys the thought of 'sucking it up'. It's like being forced to relish the taste of a dog turd served up on a platter. If you use the power of reframe and swap the word 'why' to 'what', you gain a whole new perspective of what it has served to you to deal with from the experience.

A WHY QUESTION OFTEN DENOTES AN EMOTIONAL COMPONENT TO ANSWER, OR HIGHLIGHTS A REASON OR CAUSE FOR THE MOUNTAIN LION IN YOUR FRIDGE.

In my case of cancer, I could have asked myself, 'Why would I be diagnosed with another?' But I chose to reframe instead for several reasons – let me explain. A why question denotes blame, shame and guilt immediately to the inquisitor. It infers the action of the question asker to reflect on the reason or cause. Asking myself what I could learn from the experience was a gift of untold proportions.

In my experience, cancer is little more than luck and no fault should be drawn. Yet we criticise ourselves and self-punish and talk smack to ourselves when the going gets tough at the time of diagnosis! Other than making you feel worse and completely stuck, what is this serving you? You gain absolutely nothing.

I could talk about the involvement of epigenetics, diet and the management of chronic stress in one's life – all of which contribute to cancer. There are likely to be the questions surrounding 'Why me?' but what if you were to consider what you can learn from this experience? Does that one question stop you in your 'why' tracks immediately? Did you pause and take a slow, deep breath and calm a little?

Here's the thing; if you're dealing with a big threat on your life, none of those reasons you procured inside your head matter right now. *Do they?*

Looking for the cause for the mountain lion in your fridge is causing you to look in the rear-view mirror of your life. You've already opened the fridge door and discovered the beast. It's done. It's not in your control to go back and make changes. You can't relive your life or get a do-over. But YOU can make changes.

You're not doing yourself any favours by mentally beating yourself up with all the analysis of the why. Excessive or ongoing thinking literally will drain your physical energy to maintain the mental stamina to power the brain and continue assessing what did or did not go right or wrong. The answer to overcoming the stress of a cancer diagnosis (and it's easier to implement than you think) is to ask yourself this one question.

WHAT IS IN MY CONTROL RIGHT NOW?

Sit with that question and check in with your body. Is it still in a state of flight or fight? Or perhaps are you suddenly eager to explore new horizons? Is there a shift?

Asking 'what' questions shifts your vision, motivation and drive for life forward. It changes the mindset into a solution-orientated field. One of the most empowering things you can gift yourself is to ask yourself 'what' questions. Asking yourself 'What can I learn from this experience?' literally reprograms your conscious brain into solution-seeking actions, rather than hosting a 'pity party'.

In recent interviews and public speaking events, people were astounded by my 'embrace-not-fight' approach to my cancer chapter. Society conditions you to having to *fight* cancer rather than embracing the experience. When I explained the psychological difference between the questions of *why* versus *what* that enables you to stop looking behind you and focus ahead of you, my audience had an 'Aha' moment, which empowered them to also change their mindset from uncertainty to empowerment.

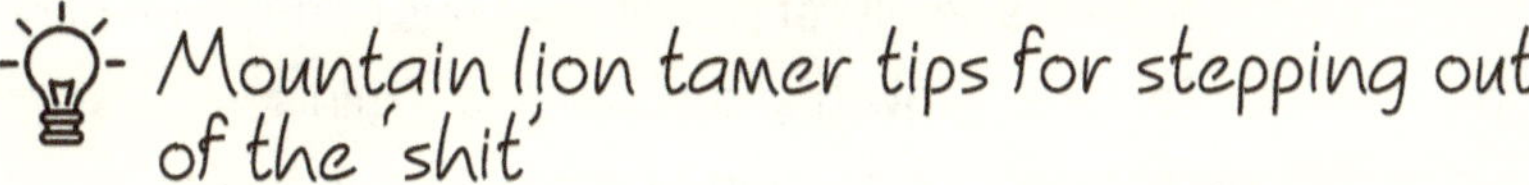

Mountain lion tamer tips for stepping out of the 'shit'

How to use affirmations:

Step 1 – Identify your chosen affirmation

Step 2 – Ask yourself in relation to the affirmation

    a.   Why is the affirmation true?

    b.   What do you do that blocks or hinders the affirmation?

    c.   What would my life be like if the affirmation were true?

    d.   What can I do every day to feel like the affirmation?

Step 3 – Answer the questions in your journal – you're telling yourself your own story from a whole new perspective.

Step 4 – Watch how your beliefs shift or watch what you now can observe after you've explored the question in your journal over several days.

Step 5 – Now repeat your daily affirmation until you're living the embodiment of the positive statement.

Be your own teacher

You're going to need to cut yourself some slack here and be patient. Become willing to accept that what arises will probably be negative thoughts and feelings (you've been shoving stuff under the carpet for years). You can choose to feel everything is negative or that every negative thing you reframe is another step closer to being a more vibrant, happy you.

Recognise that progress is small yet powerful at this early stage of healing your trauma tale. Personal growth and healing feel miniscule, yet you are recreating an entirely new foundation of how to be you. You're creating new muscle memory; you are literally reprogramming your beliefs. Believe me, this is huge.

When introducing his basic breathing method to reset the sympathetic nervous system, Wim Hof says that we are the alchemists and we are built to be in command of our own soul, light, spirit and life.

I agree with Hof. Most clients step into my clinic space as a stressed-out meerkat and need someone to hold space for them whilst they connect to their breath and then their feelings. I regularly use and record guided meditation for clients so they experience serene calm. This directly provides the client with evidence that they can achieve this state. I provide them with the recording so they can reproduce this feeling at home which empowers them to drive their own change process.

When I first met Dan, he told me he had done time in prison in his early twenties. He had enormous regret about his behaviour and worked hard now to always do the right thing. It routinely challenged Dan, causing him to feel frustrated and angry. He told me he always feels 'like he is walking on red-hot coals' especially with his ex-partner.

During his first session I used kinesiology to defuse these fiery feelings and sedate his many deep survival switches. I used guided meditation to redirect his focus from what the ex-partner had done and focus on where these feelings had been stored in his body. I guided him to shrink and release all the feels from this situation and place in his body until he could no longer visualise the stress.

At the end of the session, Dan was euphoric. First, that he was no longer invested in his ex-partner. He focused on his happiness. He now felt empowered that he could attempt to repeat this process at home anytime it triggered him.

This is the power of simple tools, such as using our breath with meditation or journalling to identify information about our shenpa. Using purposeful breath, Dan gained a conscious understanding of the feelings surrounding the traumatic event of being betrayed by a partner. He could identify the resultant undesired behaviours, including fear of trusting. With a little support, Dan could use meditation to locate the energy of the emotions and let go.

What's left is a new sense of body freedom and the experience was a gift. The healing of the trauma response is a gift which steps us into the next chapter of creating space to build upon self-worth. The objection or doubt that many people I see have is they feel so stuck that they can't heal.

Wrap-up

We've learnt that maintaining emotional responses consumes physical energy, which is maintained by stress in your mental modulation programming. You need to embrace courage and make a commitment to yourselves to activate change, and you are responsible for change occurring in your lives.

The challenge is to allow yourself to be vulnerable.

Perhaps before you expose your belly, read the next chapter regarding letting go so you're armed with a ton of strategies to move forward in your life!

In this chapter, I outlined how you process emotions. In the next chapter I will explore methods of how to let go of the negative trauma-based emotional response and activate forgiveness.

# Mountain lion tamer affirmations to sit with the feels

Big girl pants

1. Put the oxygen mask on yourself first.

2. I allow myself to remember the good times.

3. I am connected to happiness bubbles.

Have a little faith

4. I allow myself to feel nurtured and protected.

5. My thoughts are calm and I have peace of mind.

6. I choose to remain in this moment to capture the lesson.

Sit in your shit

7. It is safe for me to have feelings which easily come and go.

8. I release the need to suppress my ability to learn about myself.

9. I release all stress around remembering things.

Be your own teacher

10. I am patient and gentle with myself.

11. I am willing to heal one step at a time.

12. I now allow myself freedom to emerge from my past.

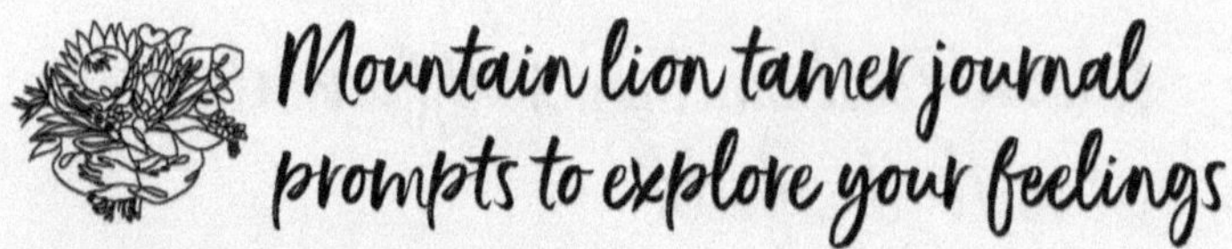

Mountain lion tamer journal prompts to explore your feelings

Big girl pants

1. Think of a situation whereby you feel like there is unfinished business and allow your feelings about this situation, event or person to arise. Now answer the following in your journal:

    a. What / who challenges you?

    b. Why does it push all the buttons?

    c. What are the actual feelings that are arising?

    d. What am I thinking / speaking to myself today?

2. How would my life be improved if I could use my feelings to learn from the past rather than repeating trauma patterns?

3. What might I need to do to feel comfortable embracing and sitting in my trigger feelings?

Have a little faith

4. Where can I be kinder to myself today?

5. Where can I ease up and give myself permission to simply allow myself to accept and release whatever feelings arise?

Sit in your shit

6. When I express my emotions with ease I feel...

7. When I open up to the energy of trust I can...

8. My potential for healing is unlimited when I...

Be your own teacher

9. Where in life can I embrace patience to be gentle with myself? What would my life look and feel like when I do this?

10. When I look at the week ahead, where can I allow myself the time for self-devotion? Is it easy to set aside time for myself, and if not, why?

11. What is my life looking like when I allow trust to bloom?

Chapter Seven

Cutting the ties

It's fine to advise someone to let go of their stuff, but the actual practice is a different story.

When I talk about 'stuff', I'm talking about that stagnant, emotional energy that is stuck in your head or body – fears, worries and all of that overthinking that you sometimes do when you're stressed. It's easy enough to say 'just let it go' flippantly, but another thing is to undertake unwinding a behavioural pattern and then laying down what stresses you out in everyday life. When you are amid a trauma response, you can't contemplate what it is you must let go of because you're too busy determining what you have to do, just to survive that moment.

To heal from the trauma, you must address the subsequent survival response you've developed. I spoke about your feelings and their impacts on your energy systems. Now I'm going to explore how you can heal your trauma response by facing the hurdles in front of you, one at a time. You need to observe and respond, and see the attachment(s) to the trauma and then learn how to cut the ties to your old reactive patterns.

We need to learn how to embrace our *shenpa*, the trigger or hook to all the emotional, mental and physical discomfort you initially experienced when you opened the fridge door and the subsequent fears you feel returning to the fridge. It's this hook that causes you to reactivate your survival response trigger. In chapter two, I discussed how this hook activates your survival switch, draining your physical energy by keeping you hypervigilant. Once that survival switch activates, it prevents you from healing from the trauma. This hook or reactivation to the traumatic event keeps you stuck in survival mode and therefore you can't thrive in life.

To thrive in life, you need to learn how to feel safe again. Having a perception of feeling safe assists you to embrace unconditional love by residing in your heart space instead of your head. Shifting out of your head and into your heart enables you to build upon your courage resources. The flow-on effect is that you naturally push your resilience boundaries further out to experience more love in your life. The more space you have to live, the more you live your life rather than simply surviving it.

University of California, Berkeley, Greater Good Science Center defines forgiveness (based on psychology) as 'a conscious, deliberate decision to release feelings of resentment or vengeance towards a person or a group who have harmed you, regardless of whether they actually deserve your forgiveness or not. Forgiveness does not mean forgetting nor does it mean condoning or excusing things done to you.'

Ellen Bass and Laura Davis, authors of *The courage to heal: A guide for women survivors of child sexual abuse*, discuss the importance of forgiveness as one of the most fundamental steps of healing the trauma response. Every author on this subject reiterates forgiveness as a necessity for healing. *You are your priority in your own life!*

One of the most profound and yet common ailments that I see and hear about from trauma clients is their feeling stuck in every facet of life. When you break down their list of ailments in conversation, in a clinic session or a workshop, the common denominator is clients are stuck in their trauma response. The consequential behavioural response patterns directly result from their survival switch being activated. The switching drives the *reaction* to everything in their life. One of the most powerful tools one can introduce into their life is *forgiveness of self*, especially how you've responded since that original trauma event.

Forgiveness enables you to re-channel the energy that you spend feeling angry or resentful regarding that trauma event – whether it be a cancer diagnosis, a fight with a loved one or being yelled at by a boss. Forgiveness gifts you the opportunity to redirect your focus back on yourself. This redirection then enables you to identify what you can do from this point on, rather than focusing on the past. I liken this process to looking forward on the road ahead of you instead of being fixated with the rear-view mirror. And just to be clear, one act of forgiveness does not clear your trauma response. This is because our lives are not one-dimensional; they are an energetic web, like connections weaved into your language of experience.

Healing your trauma tale is a process that takes time, permission and patience with yourself. It also incorporates a bunch of kindness to yourself. After all, every human being on the planet thrives on kindness.

If you're reading this book to support a loved friend or family member who has experienced a trauma, don't throw out the statement of 'Oh! *Honey, just forgive and forget, move on*'. Please try to understand that the person who is experiencing the trauma response is literally stuck in their *reaction mode* and not able to move forward. They literally can't access their tools to heal, it's all they can do to survive. This chapter might provide you with some insight, resources or even opportunities for conversation to love all over that person who is suffering in your life.

I'd like to point out that on some level, someday, you may choose to forgive the people involved in your trauma event. However, that is not for now. You are number one in your life. This chapter outlines the forgiveness tools that *you* need to heal yourself right now.

As discussed in previous chapters, as you learn to embrace your *shenpa*, that causes you to activate your trauma response trigger. You identify how your reaction can drain your physical, mental, or emotional energy stores, and prevent you from healing. I've discussed how this hook keeps you stuck and it's taking you continually to a *choice-crossroad*, whereby you choose the wrong path – the comfortable one, which doesn't focus on anything other than avoidance.

Your journey through life is not straight; it's a wiggly line. The avoidance path is a spiral that takes you straight back to a deep, dark hole in the ground. Letting go is important because it's one of the keys that enables you to feel safe again. As you embrace your trauma response, you build up the reserve of your courage resources. You push your resilience boundaries out so that instead of living your life looking at the side of a box, you can step out of the darkness and continue to move forward living your life rather than simply surviving it.

I often reference my copy of *You can heal your life* by globally renowned self-help guru Louise Hay, who attributed her life-work to the understanding that emotional trauma drives physical ailments.

In this chapter I'll be discussing the difference between fear and love. I'll introduce the concept of forgiveness not to make someone else feel better or give away your power but to lighten the load of your emotional wound. I'll also share tips on how to surrender the emotional load that you carry.

The epic battle of fear versus love

There is a difference between fear and love. It sounds obvious, I know, but they are effective opposites which are experienced in different internal locations. Only your head processes fear; your heart is the love zone.

When you're in your head you're operating fear-based emotions and subsequent neurological patterns. When you're in your heart, you feel safe and experience connections to love. I frequently explain the difference between fear and love and how they are opposites, much like Yin and Yang. A client can gain huge clarity about their trauma response when they understand consciously that fear via your subconscious has enormous impacts on their lives, including the way their body can subtly physically and mentally react.

We know the energy of love is light, and being opposite, the energy of fear is heavy and dark. Love lives in your heart's space within your physical body. The energy of love is how you thrive in life and is the fuel for your resilience. Love enables you to expand and embrace your life. Love is the natural state you are born into. Fear is the complete opposite of love.

Fear is the negativity whereby you are stuck in survival mode. Fear can cause you to not utilise your rational brain, therefore driving you to misunderstand or misinterpret sensory cues from your external world. This equates to misperception and has a direct impact on your perception of safety, trust and confidence. This affects your beliefs of being willing and capable. You lose faith in yourself which impacts your sense of self-worth.

Fear breeds fear because it is attached to the survival switch. Turn that switch on and there is no capacity for healing your emotional wound, only surviving until you feel safe again. This emotional wound makes you feel physically heavy and mentally clouded. Fear in this way cycles and continues to build within your mind. Left unchecked, fear can rapidly cause what some like to call the 'big drama' of life. No matter where you go, you're left feeling like you can't escape the drama. It's not something you shake. As Chodron claims, this *shenpa* or hook is something you need to face and deal with. Avoidance of this discomfort only causes more distress.

An example of fear-versus-love is explained beautifully by Don Miguel Ruiz in his books *The mastery of love* and *The four agreements: A Toltec wisdom book*. His second agreement states:

'DON'T TAKE ANYTHING PERSONALLY. NOTHING OTHERS DO IS BECAUSE OF YOU. WHAT OTHERS SAY AND DO IS A PROJECTION OF THEIR OWN REALITY, THEIR OWN DREAM. WHEN YOU ARE IMMUNE TO THE OPINIONS AND ACTIONS OF OTHERS YOU WON'T BE THE VICTIM OF NEEDLESS SUFFERING.'

 DON MIGUEL RUIZ 

Imagine being able to readily embrace Don's concept that what anyone says about you is none of your business? I almost laugh out loud when I quote Don in clinic, and at your likely response to reading it too – 'Yeah right, how do I do that?'

Let me explain what's going on in your big, beautiful brain to help you understand. When you have all that negativity swirling inside your mind, you are likely to experience monkey chatter that is noisy and distracting – the monkey perpetuates the survival program you're running. It's so easy to deflect from your uncomfortable feelings and blame someone externally to you. Am I right?

As you begin to embrace your *shenpa*, you are granting permission to yourself to sit in that uncomfortable triggered stuff from the trauma response. You are taking responsibility to reflect on your contribution to the situation or the lesson to be learnt from the trauma. You're also 'bitch-slapping' the monkey to shut the hell up!

This moment of reflection is a pause point. By consciously choosing to pause and connect with your breath, you dial down and can even switch off your survival program. The brain instantly switches on the frontal cortex and begins seeking solutions to take actions for you to resolve the challenge at hand. Once the brain has switched off from survival and you continue deep and purposeful breathing, you are grounding yourself, or centring, if you will. You are connecting with the energy that makes you feel stable and capable of change.

The gift of now being grounded, centred, focused and balanced means you can detach the mental energy of having things going around in your head. I liken this to stepping down from your head and into your heart space. The transition to the heart allows the love to flow to yourself as you continue to observe your feelings. What is happening is you are now curious about your trauma response rather than fearful.

In her book *A Course in Miracles*, American author, Helen Schucman states that 'our greatest power to change the world is to change your mind about the world. You have the power to change our thoughts and understanding of the world around us. From the space of bitterness and resentment to acceptance and understanding.'

YOU CAN USE CURIOSITY AS A PAUSE POINT IN YOUR LIFE THAT ENABLES YOU TO SWITCH FROM FEAR TO LOVE.

Embracing the concept that what others do is none of your business gifts you permission to shed judgement of an event or others. Shedding judgement allows you to focus on yourself and your response, rather than continuing to react. This is where the power of 'reframing' your perception becomes powerful because it forces you to ask yourself to consider a positive alternative rather than continuing to wallow in a negative one. Ultimately, response enables you to live your life on your terms in your own way, and without fear.

Laying down judgement, as suggested by Don Miguel Ruiz, frees up your physical energy that was once consumed in the brain to maintain the mental energy of the fear pattern. Releasing judgement also defuses the build up of negative emotional energy so that your energy systems can return to equilibrium. Embracing your *shenpa*, sitting with your uncomfortable, enables you to be free to love and get curious about life once more rather than remain switching with the fear program running. I relate to *practise the pause* as a gift that enables us to walk through a doorway called *opportunity*.

I can remember a day in the clinic when I was working with a great bloke, Simon. He had identified he was grieving for his dead brother after he had originally come to me for fear about uncertainty regarding the future and money.

At the end of his second session, we performed a guided meditation whereby Simon could picture himself standing in a safe space, holding an empty balloon. Part of the meditation encouraged Simon to become curious regarding all of the negative feelings we'd uncovered and defused in his session. I encouraged him to connect with these emotions and how they made him feel in his body on a physical level.

He reported feeling tension, discomfort and heaviness. Using gentle and subtle hypnotic and meditative direction, I prompted Simon to allocate more information to these feelings that he was storing on a physical level. I asked whether these feelings had a colour? A texture? Were these feelings heavy or light? How big were they? And so forth. I continued this until Simon had a crystal-clear vision of the concrete weight sitting in his chest and abdominal area.

To Simon's surprise, using the intuitive meditation, he envisioned filling a balloon with these negative feelings until it blew up! At the end of the session, much to his amazement, Simon reported feeling lighter and freer, as if he had never experienced the fear before.

To avoid overthinking the session or its components, I gave Simon homework that challenged his old habits of fear-based judgement, so that he could actively begin working towards his goals of feeling peaceful within. I instructed him that anytime he consciously discovered he was analysing anything, especially money, he was to use the following mantra, 'In this moment I am safe and well,' and then scan his body for any hidden feelings, just like we'd done in the meditation.

In subsequent sessions Simon reported now feeling extremely comfortable digging deep and readily obtaining incredible insight to challenges he has experienced. This is a profound mindset change from the anxious young man I first met who lacked self-confidence and belief in self.

Both in my personal and professional environment, I have experienced doubt that a simple meditation could shift negativity that is anchored to your core energy systems. Yet when I am able to combine techniques for multiple modalities, such as kinesiology and coaching, I can support a client to reduce the negative trauma response, which frees up the physical and mental energy within the body. I can then use meditation to enable the client to visualise removing where the trauma response is anchored. It is much like editing a movie and changing the scenery to something you desire rather than something that makes you feel uncomfortable. It's an incredible privilege to hold space for people and watch them transform their lives right in front of me.

For some people that I see, their trauma response when triggered leaves the person feeling extremely raw and vulnerable and completely out of control because of their fears consuming an incredible amount of their system energy. Experiences like sexual or physical assault leave more than just physical marks and the resultant emotional deficits require very cautious steps through the landmine of habits that may have subsequently formed. If you've experienced this type of trauma, be sure to engage a suitably qualified therapist you feel completely safe with to support you in navigating your first steps through the potentially raw minefield.

This simple technique of identifying the impact of the feelings serves several purposes. First, it enables the person to get really clear on a conscious level (even when undertaking hypnosis or meditation) of what they are feeling physically, mentally and emotionally in an acceptable and safe way.

 *Mountain lion tamer tip to release fear*

1. Make imagined balloon animals (this can be meditative).

2. Picture the trigger event.

3. Allow yourself to reconnect with the uncomfortable feelings – really feel it.

4. Grant permission to your imagination to breathe out the negative feeings.

5. Fill the balloon with all the garbage emotions and feelings.

6. Tie a knot in the metaphorical balloon.

7. Watch it float away beyond the horizon until you can't see it anymore.

Most people will attempt to explore their emotional wound but as soon as it feels uncomfortable, they run for the hills. Think of the last time you craved your favourite food. Was that process easy to overcome or did you feel pushed? Our modern society drives the quick-fix solution which causes us to shove more of our stuff under the carpet and not deal with it.

Surrender isn't failure

The Oxford Dictionary defines surrender as 'ceasing resisting'. Many people regard surrender as failure or giving up. People so often cling to adversity in the false belief that it gives you security. I provide the 'reframe' perspective of this topic by asking 'What does it cost you to hang on to all the negativity of your trauma response?' Surrender is a gift of release from deep within you. Surrender is the choice that takes you to the pause point intersection and redirects you back onto your rightful life path. The trick about surrender is that you must first grant permission on a conscious level.

Each of my teachers in my life has imparted fantastic gems, which have enabled me to learn the most valuable life lessons. One of the more profound ones, which relate so well to embracing the challenge of surrender, I learnt when I trained with the incredible Jacque Mooney. It goes like this:

IMAGINE YOU COULD SEE, AS IF FOR THE FIRST TIME, SOMEONE WHO HAS CAUSED YOU DISCOMFORT OR PAIN.

Sit with that. Read it again if you must because it's mighty powerful! Is your initial response, 'No, I can't or won't do that'? If you answered 'yes', let me tell you that anger, judgement and fear are wrestling within you to strangle your ability to think big in this moment. You're back being a dog 'poop' squished on the ground.

No one can see these feelings or emotional energy that you are holding on to. They can't see the thoughts or mental energy you invest in all that thinking and analysis. So, unless you hiss and spit at these people who push your buttons, they don't feel your wrath unless you give them the 'stink eye'! So please, I beg of you, please ask yourself – 'What am I gaining from having this negativity within me?'

I want you to imagine what it could feel like to put your trauma response, and all that hate-fire you've been clutching at, on the ground. Might your life be easier? Lighter? Freer? Remember this is your healing journey.

I'm not asking you to forget or even forgive. I'm merely asking you to assess the weight of the luggage you carry that you have stuffed full of emotional and mental energy about your perception of an experience.

There's another aspect of surrendering I would like to introduce you to, and that is accepting the realisation that not all people are capable or willing to change. You surrender your pain and negativity for yourself and your healing. Sometimes you're going to need to accept some people are noodle strainers.

I liken our journey work of healing trauma tales to Japanese kintsugi bowls. Kintsugi is the Japanese art of putting broken pottery pieces back together with gold – built on the idea that in embracing flaws and imperfections, you can create an even stronger, more beautiful piece of art. These bowls can serve hearty broth to special visitors who attend your home.

Imagine that we are all spiritual beings having a human experience and we can be represented as these beautiful and unique hand-thrown ceramic bowls – each one individual. Our experiences of life can cause chips, cracks, and flaws in the bowls – this is our humanness and perfectly normal.

Now imagine that as we actively undertake the healing of our trauma tale, we can apply gold to reseal the flaws and re-establish the purpose of the bowl to embrace and celebrate the imperfections rather than disguise the flaw (or wound). Know that some people will embrace their courage and seal up the cracks.

Also know that not everyone is willing or capable of doing this task well. Sometimes their access to self-love isn't sufficient and they run out of gold, others aren't willing to seal up the cracks. Regardless of the reason, the result is the same. The bowl with cracks can no longer hold broth, it can only strain noodles. Some people migrate through their life as a noodle strainer, unmotivated to be accountable for their behaviour after an experience. Unwilling to change or even see another perspective of their situation.

Rather than judge these people, I learnt that these are the people who require the most love of all. People who are noodle strainers are broken, stuck, lost – call it whatever you want. Their trauma tale runs their life and they aren't capable of change.

Being able to surrender to your trauma tale is ultimately a gift of self-love. It allows you to increase your capacity for both mental and emotional energy. Surrendering doesn't leave you feeling weak. Quite the opposite, in fact. Surrendering makes you feel empowered, to feel safe in exploring your behaviours and internal dialogue with a fresh set of eyes.

Being able to surrender doesn't mean giving up. I'm referring to you laying down your weapons (like the negative self-talk, the anger, the pain) and seeing the events in your life as a potential pattern. Surrendering doesn't make you weak or concede to someone else. It merely means you are ceasing your contribution to the drama that has continued to unfold since the trauma. Surrendering to the bullshit makes you an adult.

When you can review your life from a place of love and kindness, you gift yourself with several things. First, surrendering your current situation gifts you a different perspective of the original situation. Secondly, surrendering gifts you a bigger view of how you currently perceive reality – because when you're in survival mode, it's like wearing goggles and your peripheral vision gets shut out.

Surrendering gifts you the conscious awareness that, up to this point, whilst trying to stay safe, you have done the best you can. Now that you feel safe enough to explore the scenarios a little more, a little deeper or clearer, perhaps you can gain insight and wisdom about yourself and others? For example, *I wonder what happened to that person to cause them to become a noodle strainer?'*

Granting yourself permission to surrender can be like giving yourself the biggest Christmas present you have ever received. It can be life-changing. This is a gift of awareness and knowledge that enables you to consider taking different actions. Surrendering is like stepping out of the fishbowl you call life – it allows you to get a very clear picture of the stress associated with a situation, gain an understanding of your reactive response, and gain insight into what may have caused the other person to behave as they did.

This awareness allows you to feel the connection between your feelings and the physical impact on your body at a conscious level. This new-found wisdom enables you to make a conscious and different choice about your future behaviour and, therefore, drive your healing and change processes within your brain.

Powerful, right? Probably uncomfortable, but again that's on you and how you choose to perceive your healing. Keep referencing the powerful mantra by Louise Hay, *everything in front of me is good*. Even when something is crappy, you can change your mindset about nearly any experience.

What if you could just surrender to all this awareness without beating yourself up? Would life not be simpler? Would that allow you then to connect with your internal happiness barometer? Does this or that make me happy? If not, stop doing it!

We are not gifted life to punish ourselves – we're here to experience as much joy as humanly possible. Use the tools to break the cycle of your trauma tale!

What if you could just accept that you've done the best you can over the years? What if you could surrender to the whole stinking chaos within you? And before you even spend a millisecond beating yourself up now you know better, what if you could simply celebrate – now I know better, I can do better.

Now you realise that your old patterns of behaviour and thinking no longer serve you. It's okay to admit it's time for a change!

Beth is a social worker. Raised in a religious family, Beth experienced a traumatic childhood when her father became mentally unstable, ceased taking his meds, and left his family. She was just a child yet processed this abandonment as her fault. The subsequent survival program that imbedded within Beth referenced to a fear of failure, jealousy, insecurity and need for control.

In a powerful session, she set her goal to feel safe, secure and connected to herself. Initially, she fought with me regarding the need to analyse and understand as much information as she could regarding her triggers and what that may refer to.

As the session continued, we defused more stress and uncovered how intricately the stress-based survival pattern had woven into her behaviours. Beth realised she didn't need to understand everything. She could connect to the energy she'd invested in analysis and overthinking, and further connected this to the defensive behaviour that was causing her to sabotage her stability. We celebrated her acknowledgement that she overanalysed anything and got stuck in that mental space in her head. We laughed when she admitted the overanalysis made her a noodle strainer!

The most powerful component of that session was Beth's awareness of her connection to her 'relaxed self'. She could then lay down the trigger behaviours, allowing the energy of that to dissipate.

Now she had energy to decide to become her own parent, and nurture herself. As the parent she can now 'decide to be safe in any moment', she can step away when triggered to recentre herself. She could lay down the need to analyse and control everything and simply accept her triggered feelings are remnants of the old survival pattern.

Don't be arrogant enough to think you can read the suggested action of 'lay down' your troubles and they will disappear. I am muffling a 'Snoopy-snigger' because I wanted this once too. I was so desperate to be rid of the negativity. I wanted to shift it all at once. What I realise is that I would have missed many valuable lessons along the way. I would not have understood how intricately woven some behavioural patterns had knitted within my body or thought processes.

Learning to surrender is a courageous process of defusing a lifetime of stress-based behaviours and emotional attachment to running survival programs. It takes bravery to pause a survival program, so simply tell yourself – 'Enough already!' Laying down the luggage that you've been carrying around is not an act of weakness. Defusing this type of stress is like untangling a ball of Christmas lights. You don't just pull the lights out of the box and they are simply ready to hang. You have to unravel them, test that the globes still work and check for exposed wires.

 Mountain lion tamer tip to let go

1. Practise permission.

    a. It's okay to sit in the moment, and remind yourself to breathe and recentre yourself, get grounded.

b. It's okay to remind yourself that you are safe in this moment.

c. It's okay to remind yourself that thoughts and feelings are designed to come and go, not remain stagnant within your head.

d. It's okay to detach from a trigger person or space and regroup and just do you for a while.

e. It's okay to be the adult in your life and parent your wounded child.

f. Explore aspects of yourself without judgement.

2. Try a new filter to perceive your world.

a. Don't run from the triggers, sit with your *shenpa*.

b. Simply allow yourself another five minutes of sitting with the trigger feeling.

c. Remind yourself, 'In this moment I am okay.'

d. Ask yourself, 'Do I need to analyse these feelings right now or simply lay them down?'

e. Ask yourself, 'What awareness can I learn about myself right now?'

f. Imagine seeing the trigger event through a new lens. What might you learn about yourself?

3. Shelve the problem.

a. Practise the pause.

b. Gift yourself a count of ten.

c. Time out – remove yourself from a trigger situation to catch your breath.

Wrap-up

In this chapter, we've explored the difference between fear and love and how this impacts us physically, emotionally, mentally and energetically. I have defined the meaning of true forgiveness and how this can be a wonderful gift firstly to ourselves and then others. The wonderful gift of no longer carrying the baggage of our trauma response and opening ourselves up to opportunities of thriving in life.

Finally, I explored what it is to surrender or let go of everything you have attached to your trauma response, like anger and fear. Accept my challenge that I gift you now to imagine if you could see someone as if for the first time. We've explored ways to imagine what it could feel like to put your trauma and all that hate-fire on the ground, as well as learning to accept some people are noodle strainers!

Some people often expect that letting go is simple. What they cannot recognise is it they have to be prepared to explore all the trauma response stuff that has made them feel uncomfortable and they've shoved under the carpet. Be prepared to do the work and stick with it until you feel lighter. This is often challenging alone and you can benefit from kickstarting this process with a trained professional.

In the next chapter I will explore how to pull together all the resources presented so far and migrate out of your trauma response into a space of self-worth and self-love for ultimate healing.

 # Mountain lion tamer affirmation to embrace love

Fear vs Love

1. I wish my life would be different if I was immune to the opinions of others.

2. How is my truth personal to me?

3. If I judged myself less, how would my life change?

4. If I could allow my life to be transformed, what would be possible?

5. Where can I let go of the need to change others when I am in my trauma response?

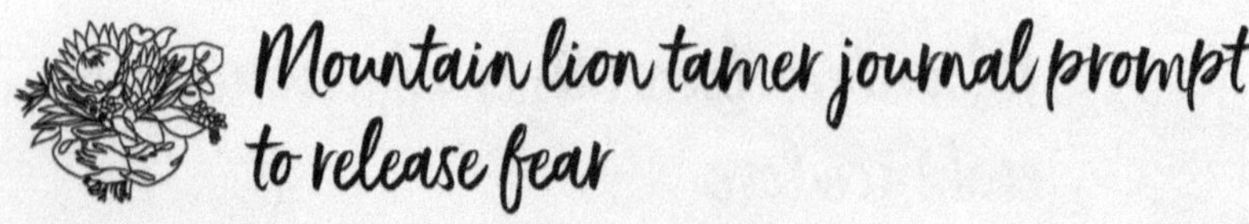 *Mountain lion tamer journal prompt to release fear*

Fear vs Love

1. What am I fearful of?

   a. How would my life be different if I could face the fear?

   b. How would my life be different if I could let go of that fear?

2. How would my life be different if I didn't take anything personally?

3. What if there was no problem in this moment?

Chapter Eight

Learning to love again

Our energy, attention and focus reside in one of two places — fear or love.

In this chapter, I will define self-worth and explain why people step on it! It's time to talk about the difference between fear and love. We also need to explore what true forgiveness is, and how this affects our ability to love ourselves. I'll also set out a challenge (should you choose to accept it), which can empower you to surrender to your trauma response and return to your heart space where your self-love lives.

These emotions and states of being are complete opposites of each other. To heal our trauma tale, you need to anchor your energy within love and this means your emotional heart space.

When you are in survival mode and stuck in your trauma response, your energy and emotions are swirling around inside your head, not your heart. There is no capacity for love when the bossy bitch called 'fear' is in town. This causes you to flit between the space of your head and your heart without consistency and it feels like you're bouncing around in a pinball machine. This generates internal chaos and is often how you lose your footing, from being grounded, centred and anchored, in your natural state of humanness – worthy and loveable.

During my initial treatment for breast cancer, I experienced terrible shame and my self-love diminished incredibly. After all, how does a natural therapies practitioner and health coach get cancer in the first place? I judged myself harshly after hearing gossip that my cancer reflected my inability to support others.

The myriad of thoughts and feelings doing laps inside my head included that I did not deserve to put myself first, which was linked to a pattern of fear of rejection. When I worked through this with my therapist, I realised in fact I had sustained an incredible amount of high-volume stress for more than a decade. My partner had experienced a workplace spinal injury. An incident pertaining to my daughter's safety had arisen, which had rocked me to the core. My mum had died and whilst I dealt with her transition well, she left a gaping hole from her role of being the stability conduit for my entire family. Whilst this is life, when it's happening all at once and you're running your own business, it's stressful. At the time I thought I was just 'busy'. I didn't have time to reflect that I was running on fumes and not self-caring anywhere near enough.

Each week, my daughter and I pick a day to have some time out and debrief how the week is going. We were at our favourite local coffee shop the week I'd been diagnosed with breast cancer. Even though my world was completely insane with worry, thoughts and logistics, I remained determined to be a mum.

I knew my daughter was terrified about everything too and putting on a brave face; we both desperately needed to connect. We needed something from our routine to remain normal, which would make us both feel safe.

Sitting in our beloved seat in the warm sunshine, sipping on our drinks and tapping forks as we pretended to fight over cake, our conversation began. My daughter poured her heart out and asked me all the questions that had been festering within her.

Normally I'm quite oblivious to anyone around me when I'm with my girl, especially in our debrief space at the coffee shop. She is my entire focus. During this occasion, I will be the first to admit the diagnosis had me frazzled, and I was still emotionally numb from the biopsy entrapment the week prior. It took all my energy to maintain my attention and focus on our conversation.

I was peripherally aware of a group of women sitting close by and attempted to remain engaged in what my twelve-year-old daughter was asking me. I remember feeling a little vague and confused when my girl stopped talking altogether; she had paused mid-sentence, with tears welling in her eyes.

I suddenly overheard what these women were saying. There was no subtlety, no filters. No consideration for who might hear what they were saying. It was just gossip, and we heard everything. I didn't know these people and they were talking about a local kinesiology practitioner who had been diagnosed with cancer.

They were gossiping about me, a complete stranger.

Now, I'm all for people saying whatever they want about me. But I'm human, so when I hear someone talking smack about me, I respond emotionally. Normally if I have heard something on the grapevine, I will reflect on what has been said to determine if I can make self-improvements and attempt to rectify any issues with interpersonal relationships.

In that moment I felt like I was back in the biopsy machine – trapped, powerless, with no voice. My inside voice was screaming, 'Are you fucking serious?' and my body was unconsciously rising out of my chair, ready to run.

I turned from these women who were now looking at me quizzically, to discover my daughter had tears streaming down her face. She was utterly devastated. My tender grasp on reality snapped and my 'mamma bear' exploded into action, gathering my girl as I stood.

'Come on, honey, we'll get our drinks to go,' I said as I stood and spoke to the beautiful staff.

I heard these women scoff and defensively question what my problem was. I ignored it in that moment. My daughter, who has inherited my fire, turned around and said, 'You're talking about my mum.'

The staff who had witnessed this incident quickly bundled up our order and gave me a hug. As we were leaving, I embraced my daughter and thanked her for her unconditional love. I turned to these women and said, 'I hope you never have to be in a position to take your child to your favourite chill zone and describe what a mastectomy is. I hope that the next time you decide to talk about someone you don't know that you could dig deep within yourself and say whatever it is you have to say with reverence and love, not fear or lack of understanding of my situation. And while you're at it, grow some balls and say it to the person's face so you can see how destructive and hurtful your words actually are.'

That encounter set my daughter and me off into a tailspin, and we returned home, both of us in tears. We reflect often about our words and how they are spoken. It was a valuable teaching moment for my girl to learn how to step outside of someone's language and get grounded. Yes, the gossip was painful to hear, but it didn't define who we are. I reframed the strangers' conversation to my daughter and told her, 'I can only hope that they are all well and have positive conservations about cancer and people's mental health from this point on. Perhaps that is the gift we gave them, honey.'

It's safe to say that the decade in the lead-up to my diagnosis was high-end stressful. I am a high vibe energy bunny, and I've learnt that living and working at that pace is not sustainable. So, when the biopsy incident occurred, the stress of that pushed me right over the edge of my mental health. I felt like my life had come to a grinding halt and I completely disconnected from who I was. I was stuck in survival mode. The café encounter was just another log on the shitstorm fire.

The time that I've had off work during surgery recovery and oncology treatment has gifted me the opportunity to disconnect from virtually everything external to myself. Perhaps my entire life I have been able to make myself the priority with no excuse or reason. I believe that is because I can say with my hand on my heart I truly love myself and I am worthy of that love and attention I can now gift to myself. What I learnt and have come to appreciate is the importance of loving self not only to make sure life is enjoyable but also to fast-track your healing process from trauma. In fact, it's a fundamental step to feeling, being and knowing you are okay.

Embracing your love and worth enables you to master your world, turn on the light in that hole you're in, and shine brightly. Embracing love for yourself activates your desire and a momentum for healing.

Create a worthy self

What is the difference between love and fear? The Oxford Dictionary defines fear 'as an unpleasant emotion caused by the threat of danger, pain, or harm'. It defines love as 'a great interest and pleasure in something'. The energy of fear operates within our head, whereas love resides within our heart space. According to Don Miguel Ruiz, there are four steps to the mastery of love and can be easily summarised when you are prepared to become aware of your fears, which block your happiness.

Through mastering your awareness, you transform to proactively taking actions, and breaking down your reactions that keep the survival switch turned on. As you clear out fears, you can view and align to the energy of love of life, through to a divine love of self whereby you become one with God or the universe. To achieve self-love, you can explore Don Miguel Ruiz's advice and implement the four agreements of life:

1.   Be impeccable with your word.

2. Don't take anything personally.

3. Don't make assumptions.

4. Always do your best.

Each of these agreements is subtly encouraging you to detach from your external world and simply focus on yourself. For example, noticing the language that you use with yourself, especially when feeling raw and vulnerable, in my experience is critical. During episodes of your trauma tale is when you especially require attention to being kind and loving to yourself.

When migrating through your day, observe the experiences, the things that you see or do, rather than judge them. Often when in a heightened state of your survival switch it is incredibly challenging to observe others, as you can be so focused on every little nuance in your own life. Being outwardly observant forces you to take that purposeful breath I spoke about in chapter three. This has been especially true during the pandemic when the conversation topic hasn't changed in 18 months!

When other people are behaving in certain ways, don't invest in their process or make assumptions, simply observe and get curious whether anything of your behaviour is being reflected back to you. The best form of kindness one can give oneself, regardless of whether you're healing from an event or not, is to accept that you're always doing your best and that if you're not, make the appropriate changes and modifications.

I love talking to people about their definitions of love, which vary for everyone based on their beliefs, values and experiences. Shame researcher and author Brené Brown discusses love as 'a feeling like you fit somewhere and you belong'. Brown distinguishes however that fitting into a group, a place or action requires you to change and modify who you are. Whereas belonging is entirely up to you because you define who you want to be and accept yourself for it. Brown reiterates that love is uncertain and you know what it is but often it's difficult to put into words. But then again, fear is the same. Brown defines love in the following way:

'We cultivate love when we allow our most vulnerable and powerful selves to be deeply seen and known, and when we honor the spiritual connection that grows from that offering with trust, respect, kindness and affection. Love is not something that we give or get, it is something that we nurture and grow, a connection that can only be cultivated between two people when it exists within each one of them – we can only love others as much as we love ourselves. Shame, blame, disrespect, betrayal and the withholding of affection damage the roots from which love grows. Love can only survive these injuries if they are acknowledged, healed and rare.'

— BRENÉ BROWN

Let's marry Brown's and Ruiz's principles together. Imagine yourself in a safe place where you could allow the defence walls down and allow yourself to feel vulnerable, standing outside of your comfort zone. Instead of feeling fear, you felt excitement to try something new without concern about not achieving perfection the first go.

Imagine that safe place was inside of you in your emotional heart space. Imagine now that you gave yourself permission to really listen to what you say to yourself. Is your language love- or fear-based? When you first explore your language, it may surprise you to hear a lot of negative or even a lot of smack talk! Don't fall into the trap of punishing yourself for doing this. We all do it.

I find the trick to not punishing yourself is to allow yourself to observe your own internal language without judgement. This is a very gentle form of surrender and acknowledgement of your stuff! Bravo! Being willing to look at yourself like this is a big step in your healing process. Bringing this awareness into your consciousness gifts you the opportunity to connect with your accountability.

If your first response language doesn't ring the positivity bell, don't fret. To change the thought/word from a negative context, simply take a purposeful breath and state, *'CANCEL THAT!!'* Follow this by immediately reframing the statement into something positive.

Saying aloud 'cancel' is like telling the universe and every cell of your body, 'Oops, I really didn't mean that!' In my experience, there is an initial and sometimes overwhelming wave of negative word vomit that you pick yourself up on and then reframe. It's okay, remember to be nice to yourself! Remind yourself that we all word vomit from time to time! After a little while, you notice that everything you say to yourself is ultra-positive. Before you realise it, you're helping others reframe their smack talk too. Alternatively, you're stepping out of conversations that contain negative energy like the news on the TV!

You are the only one truly tuned in to your energy systems. You need to trust yourself. Your energy systems have everything you need to embrace all that you are so that you're able to live the fulfilled life you want. The power of reframing your internal language is a simple yet immensely powerful tool. Remember the goal of healing your trauma tale is to trust and to be kind.

Expanding your energy using love and positivity offers you the room to grow into a newer version of yourself. When you experience the sensation of love instead of feeling fear, the energy of excitement can evolve to enable you to try something new without concern about not achieving perfection the first go.

To empower clients to feel safe and trust that they have within them all the innate abilities to heal, I often take them through a meditation exercise whereby they use their breath and grounding tools to recognise and connect with their feelings in their physical body. Without realising it, we so often disconnect from these sensations as a form of defence when we activate the survival switch. This type of guided meditation is the physical version of reframing your internal dialogue, it's just using a different energetic program.

Once relaxed and connected to their breath, I encourage the client to identify where this negative energy is in their body. Harnessing our conscious imagination is just like utilising Jedi mind tricks – the client gets to connect with where the stress is stored in their body. I invite the client to get curious about the stress – what is its shape, density, texture and colour. Once they are very clear, you can use breath and visualisation to defuse the stress and let it go. I've never had a client not be able to perform this exercise without success. From young kids, teens, adults and elderly. Everyone benefits from the use of prompts and a quickie guided meditation. Who doesn't like a quickie?

Sometimes the client struggles to imagine shifting the stress within their body because they are so stuck in their head. They consumed all their energy, maintaining a mental energy pattern. When this happens, we revisit the relaxation techniques and the contextual intention of what their session is about – for example to love yourself more, or to feel calm. Once they are calm, the client more readily comes to visualise shifting their unwanted feelings.

There is no limitation to where someone's imagination can take them. For example, they can place their crap feelings into a balloon and blow it up or let it go. Sometimes I encourage them to throw the crap into a fire or place it into a paper boat and watch it sail away. At the completion of the release process, I guide you to backfill the void that was consumed with negativity with golden light. Sometimes this is gold, much like a kintsugi bowl.

Preparing this chapter, I researched Brené Brown's book *The gift of imperfection: Let go of who you think you're supposed to be and embrace who you are: Your guide to a wholehearted life*. In this wonderful book Brown discusses that 'love and belonging are essential to the human experience'. I would expand on this concept and recommend you learn to let go of what others think. No one can ever truly understand what happens inside you, so their opinion is literally their unresolved stuff that swirls around inside them leaking out their mouth. If someone is talking smack about you, it's a reflection of where they are at, rather than about you. Others are entitled to an opinion, just like you.

Letting go of external opinion creates space for you to connect to your own story and purpose. Connection with who you really are from the perspective of your heart space is where you gain a connection to your worth. Addressing all that word vomit is a lovely way to create space to feel good in your life.

So many authors refer to how people actively avoid our lessons in life. Some call it *shenpa* (the uncomfortable), or emotional baggage or negative stuff. Everyone calls it something different, but the more you read about or discuss this topic, it beomes clear that energetically it's pretty much all the same. The Brown quote below sums up the point I'm trying to make in relation to you stepping back or disconnecting from your external world, so that it enables you to focus on self and your capacity to love who you really are.

> 'WHEN WE SPEND OUR LIFETIME TRYING TO DISTANCE OURSELVES FROM THE PARTS OF OUR LIVES THAT DON'T FIT WITH WHO WE THINK WE'RE SUPPOSED TO BE, WE STAND OUTSIDE OF OUR STORY AND HUSTLE FOR OUR WORTHINESS BY CONSTANTLY PERFORMING, PERFECTING, PLEASING AND PROVING.'

— BRENÉ BROWN

Remember back in chapter six I spoke about your thoughts, feelings and attitudes? To love yourself, you need to connect with how you are feeling in this present moment. Remaining tethered to the memory of a feeling, thought, or attitude from the past, or fear or worry about something in the future, does not serve you right now in this present moment. Brown's research clearly defined that a person's sense of belonging goes hand in hand with love. Brown refers to 'the human desire to be part of something larger than us'.

Let me ask you this – How well do you belong to your life? How well do you walk your journey path and honour your humanness? This perception and human need for belonging is far greater than your trauma response will ever be. I can only hope that this statement alone may be enough for you to pay attention to your potential word vomit and practise the reframe exercise! Being able to recognise and understand the enormity of our perfect imperfect life supported me to step out of my trauma response, and into a neutral space of simple and humble self-acceptance.

OUR LIVES ARE FILLED WITH EXPERIENCES – GOOD, BAD AND NEUTRAL.

Recognising life events as a series of experiences reduces the negative emotional charge that you hold on to or you have placed on a trauma event. Being able to reframe life as a series of experiences gets you another step closer to easily diffusing your negative traumatic survival response.

Don't get caught in the trap of 'what-ifs' of a particular time or action to measure your worth. Decide right now that your intention is to be worthy now. Decide today – now, in fact – that you are deserving and worthy of love. Because if not now, when? If not now, you risk running the rest of your life waiting for *your worth* to drop into your lap, and unfortunately tomorrow never comes. What happens is you run a thought-based program of reaction to a future time frame which does not reference the present time.

 **Mountain lion tamer tips to embrace love**

1. Close-up mirror work.

   a. Look just into your own eyes (the doorway to your soul).

   b. Utilise affirmations and say them to your reflection and allow yourself to embrace any arising feelings.

2. Begin thinking of love as an *action* rather than just a *feeling*.

   a. Allows you to assume accountability and responsibility for how you feel in the moment.

   b.   Allows you time to be gentle with yourself as you consciously become aware of negative thought patterns and dialogue.

3.   Pay attention to your self-language and where necessary reframe to something neutral or positive.

4.   Practise the pause.

   a.   Each time you become aware of a negative thought or feeling, allow yourself to pause.

   b.   You're allowed to experience the full spectrum of emotions, just don't beat yourself up for having the negative aspects, allow them to keep moving.

5.   Gift yourself a count of ten and use your breath.

I often see clients after they have seen every other imaginable practitioner there is. They tell me I am their last stop on the road. What I see is people who are genuinely wanting to help themselves, however, they have become so stuck in avoiding their *shenpa* that they destroyed their road map and can no longer navigate their way free of their trauma tale. My role as a change facilitator is to diffuse the stress on their road map so that they find their way back to their path. It's also to bring about a conscious awareness of where a person is stuck so that they can make choices that enable them to resonate from their heart space and love all over themselves.

True forgiveness

Let us explore what true forgiveness is, how it is a gift and how that gift starts with you. Healing trauma always contains a starting point of acknowledgement, followed by forgiveness. In my experience, it begins with you deciding and setting your intention to change. That change of direction often begins when you are ready to forgive yourself. Healing requires you to forgive the thoughts that you felt, the language that you've used against yourself, and basically how you've treated yourself like crap in response to a traumatic event.

FORGIVENESS BEGINS WITH YOU. BECAUSE YOU DESERVE IT.

As Louise Hay says, 'we are born as little babies loving ourselves unconditionally and somewhere along the way in our early childhood we cease doing this'. We shut down the kindness to ourselves and others and the nasty, spiteful negative behaviour ensues.

The other person doesn't feel your hate-fire, frustration, anger or rage. You're only punishing yourself with those negative thoughts and feelings. Forgiveness is an individual process which must be decided on at a conscious level. Therefore, it is intentional. I define forgiveness as an internal process of release, which I liken to dropping luggage that is full of fresh dog shit. The luggage stinks. It's heavy, and it's a burden to carry around.

Forgiveness is therefore that letting go of 'yuck' feelings. It's the dissolving of thoughts associated with emotions such as resentment, bitterness, anger and fear. When these feelings escalate and push you to breaking point, you risk wearing convict orange, because of the associated need for vengeance and retribution towards someone who you perceive has wronged us. Guess what? All of us can have these feelings about ourselves and it's called 'talking smack about yourself'! For example, when was the last time you called yourself an idiot or dickhead?

New York Times labelled motivational speaker, life coach and author Gabrielle Bernstein the next generation guru. In her book, *Add more '-ing' to your life*, Bernstein discusses that resentment is a red flag that love is missing in your life because of an old story you're telling yourself from a previous experience. I like this link of a past emotion affecting you in the present moment and it provides another reference to *shenpa*. Remember I spoke about how a survival switch is activated? I spoke about how when our amygdala in the brain activates the survival program? It is neurologically linked to our short- and long-term memory programs.

This means that you lay down a perception of an experience into your memory without your brain quantifying whether the perception is something real, something imagined, or created as your defensive response to a trauma. Fast-forward to present time, when you've triggered an emotional response, retrieving the negative feeling (here comes the *shenpa*) and simply recalling an illusionary perception of the past, rather than a known fact about your present. It is these perceptions that fill your metaphorical emotional baggage that you carry around. It is this baggage that then influences as subsequent behaviour now and in the future, unless you choose to place the luggage on the ground and let it go.

IT IS TIME TO STOP PUNISHING YOURSELF WITH THIS OLD NEGATIVE REACTION.

Therefore, forgiveness is the letting go or release component of that which you've been hanging on to. This release process is how you reframe from negative to positive. It's how you create the energy to become willing to receive change in your life. It is the process which leads you to joy and peace within.

One of the most gentle and delightful forgiveness mechanisms I've used is known as *Ho'oponopono*.

The Hawaiian prayer practice of *ho'oponopono* is a gentle and loving method to sever the ties to the negative within you. It's a chant – 'I'm sorry. Please forgive me. Thank you. I love you.' Simple right? Powerful? Absolutely!

It is a subtle way of bringing consciousness to where you've processed an event or person as negative. It's a statement ultimately of forgiveness (for you), which enables you to defuse the energy associated with your negative behavioural response to the incident or person. In his *Psychology Today* article, 'The Hawaiian secret of forgiveness', President of Kona University Matt James explains that *ho'oponopono* can help anyone to let go of resentment.

> 'THE HAWAIIAN WORD *HO'OPONOPONO* COMES FROM *HO'O* (TO MAKE) AND *PONO* (RIGHT). THE REPETITION OF THE WORD *PONO* MEANS DOUBLY RIGHT OR BEING RIGHT WITH BOTH SELF AND OTHERS. IN A NUTSHELL, *HO'OPONOPONO* IS A PROCESS BY WHICH WE CAN FORGIVE OTHERS TO WHOM WE ARE CONNECTED.'

— MATT JAMES —

I tried this prayer when I was experiencing horrific PTSD anxiety. What I came to learn about the prayer is this – all my thoughts, feelings, attitudes are my responsibility. Therefore, if any of this emotional energy was negative, then the responsibility was on me to resolve the subsequent negativity that surely flowed into my body.

Step 1: *Repentance.* Recognise that you own everything inside your head. Every thought, feeling or reaction you have, to everything within and around you, it's all yours, honey! It's your responsibility. The easiest way to not punish yourself for this is to let it go. You do this by simply saying: *I'M SORRY*.

Step 2: *Ask Forgiveness*. When you seek forgiveness, do it as often as you can – your inner child is always listening and your physical body can feel the energy of remorse (which feels like letting go and surrendering all the negativity like anger and resentment you've been holding on to within yourself). The universal intention really focuses on you hearing your own words and resonating with the energy of repentance. Start with yourself and being sorry for feeling lost or stuck. Sorry for your trauma response. Continue to say it to as many people as you need to say it to! So, ask for forgiveness by simply saying: *PLEASE FORGIVE ME*.

Step 3: *Gratitude*. A person can be grateful for just about anything in their life. You can be grateful for our bodies getting you from A to B. Be grateful for doing the very best that you can. In the context of this exercise, be grateful for your conscious awareness of what you are feeling emotionally and physically. As soon as you begin the first two steps, you literally can't continue to hang on to anything negative. The rock-hard, stone-like negativity melts like chocolate. To express your gratitude for commencing the release process, simply say: *THANK YOU*.

Step 4: *Love*. This last step of saying 'I love you' enables you to step out of all the emotional and mental chaos of your head and down into your heart space. If you're having trouble finding something to love, start with the air you breathe. Love the sky. Adore the warmth from the sun. Love that you have a house. Love there are roads to drive on. Start simple and build up as you practise the exercise. Simply say: *I LOVE YOU*.

With my experience of entrapment PTSD I initially felt so humiliated. How does a coach lose her voice and become unable to speak her truth? I punished myself with my thoughts and feelings. My internal dialogue was self-loathing and detrimental. I constantly felt inadequate.

My reflection of my breast cancer chapter highlighted my inability to step off the treadmill of negativity and survival. This was because of ongoing triggers to my sensory system whilst attending oncology treatment. The sounds and smells of the oncology ward, the gowned staff, the lighting, all subtly replicated that biopsy day. It wasn't until I began working with my therapist that I came to realise I had been very harsh with myself.

My expectations for my healing were beyond unreasonable. My therapist suggested that I try guided meditation to reframe my mindset with *Ho'oponopono* prayer. With this activity I soon thrived by picturing myself as a parenting adult for myself. I began dialoguing with my own inner child. When I could visualise the pain that a version of myself was holding on to, i.e. my inner child, I could feel compassion and empathy for myself once again.

With the use of the prayer and meditation, I began my return to being able to love myself once more. I could forgive myself for the paralysis I experienced. I could forgive myself for the thoughts that had arisen from that biopsy day. I was able to lay down the negativity that I subsequently experienced to free up space and settle back into my heart.

I realise through nearly two decades of work that whilst people benefit from therapy over a period, the healing process can be significantly expanded and fast-tracked when they are willing and able to implement small, positive actions at home. When a client is proactive with their healing homework, they are creating so much more than new positive habits.

When a person chooses to empower themselves with forgiveness (starting with themselves), they are consciously diffusing negativity caused by stress from survival programs they have been running. I can always tell when a client has made this decision and taken the required action. When they return for their follow-up sessions, you can then dig deeply, and often to the root cause of where a survival pattern has begun.

All too often people have an expectation or a perception that it is difficult or hard to forgive. I attribute this to the stress signal having infiltrated their values and beliefs into thinking that the process is hard and external to themselves.

When you have a breakthrough moment with your therapist and can experience that pure reconnection to heart space, you come to realise that the weight of the negativity you've been carrying is now pointless and forgiveness is your only joyous option. That breakthrough moment whereby you feel light and free of the emotional luggage is when you shake off the cloak of victimhood.

The moral of the story is this – you can only do you in your life. Stop playing it safe! Stop beating yourself up! Start being brave. Start adulting yourself, instead of waiting for someone else to do it. Learn to forgive the steps that you've taken to get you where you are today. This can start by ceasing the 'smack talk'.

Some people have something to gain from remaining negative. It's called secondary gain. By this I mean that on some unconscious level they perceive they gain a reward from not changing, not healing, not growing, and not evolving in their life. These people outwardly appear to survive on emotions of spitefulness, resentment, and vengeance. In fact, they are stuck in the mental energy of their emotions. You could liken that to emotional pain body. You can't judge those who are incapable of change, but you can forgive them for being so stuck that their only option is to remain in that space of victimhood.

For people running secondary gain patterns, choice and behaviours, this is the best that they can do. Is it right? Probably not, but who am I to judge?

The other noteworthy point is that when you step out of victimhood and begin the forgiveness process, you can experience a lot of change within yourself. You may perceive that those around you are not changing, and this can push your buttons as well! This perception can send you straight back to the patterns that you have been working on forgiving yourself for – shame, blame, guilt, anger and resentment. The more you allow yourself to become consciously aware, the more you can activate forgiveness within yourself.

REMEMBER THAT YOU'RE NOT RESPONSIBLE FOR CHANGING ANYONE BUT YOURSELF.

Finally, I have no expectation that you could or would want to forgive anyone who has perpetrated something against you. Straight up. Gift yourself forgiveness first, understanding and kindness, for holding any negativity within you. Your job is to heal and to love your trauma response. It's challenging to do either of those things with suitcases of emotional baggage swinging off you.

This sort of self-development and healing work isn't something you simply 'fit in' whilst the kids are outside playing. It's a dedication and requires commitment to regularly touching base and checking in with yourself.

Love the inner child

So many people ask me, 'What is the inner child'? It's the culmination of your childhood experiences and feelings whilst you were neurologically soft-wired. Soft-wired relates to the period between conception and seven years of age. It's a combination of genetic expression and environmental conditions, i.e. your family. It's a time whereby your soul is not yet imbedded in the physical body and you're unconsciously gathering references of how to live your life.

Whilst you are soft-wired, you develop the part of you that experiences all the firsts in your life. This is the part of you that holds the root cause of your trauma response that you are still living out. Your inner child holds the key or magnet to your shame, blame and guilt patterns.

So how do you connect with your inner child? It's quite simple. You do what makes you fucking happy! The inner child version of you is the keeper of all the raw from your first experiences. They hold the wound, and this is the part of you that requires healing. Your inner child also holds the key to your heart space and the capacity to experience pure joy.

A child doesn't understand why negative things happen. A child just wants to be loved and to experience joy. Even into adulthood, there is still a part of us that is childlike. It's how we connect to simple pleasures of joy. Reflect on how your body has an electrical and neurological memory of every experience.

Modern society is leading us down a path of disconnection from ourselves. By this I mean we are rarely connected to our emotions or how we are physically feeling. When you experience trauma, you become disconnected from your heart space and your body. You connect to your thoughts about what happened and therefore become stuck in your head.

Louise Hay, author of *You can heal your life*, gave rise to the concept of the inner child. I interpret that as your brain records your early messages whilst you are soft-wired. Louise explains we believe everything in our life to be true and this period of your life establishes the foundation of how you solidify your values and beliefs. Whenever you blame someone else, you are not taking responsibility for yourself. You can't forgive yourself without empowering the child within you who holds all the raw experiences.

After my entrapment within the biopsy machine, when I'd lost my voice, my inner child was screaming at me, at the situation, and at life. I was foetal on the floor with PTSD after that experience and my inner child was demanding my attention – because she was hurting deeply.

I tried my normal breathing techniques but still I had anxiety, nightmares and flashbacks. I tried grounding constantly and whilst I felt somewhat calmer, I still suffered from unbearable anxiety. I revisited guided meditation, this time with a meditation teacher who taught me how to simply reside in my heart space. BAM! My inner child appeared and demanded my attention.

Losing my voice during and after the entrapment experience linked me back to another time in my life whereby I had shut down memories of trauma. The correlation to literally feeling stuck, disempowered, alone, and frightened all returned.

The results were so dramatic that I enrolled in an Intuitive Meditation for Kinesiology Practitioners and learnt how to combine the two modalities to support me to listen whilst in my trauma tale, acknowledge and release where I hadn't been loving myself.

Through meditation, I could see and hear my inner child and process the emotions that the adult version had become stuck on. Using meditation, I could feel safe on my terms. I could nurture my child. It was like granting permission to myself to become my own parent, capable of nurturing and nourishing the broken pieces within myself.

Those broken pieces included the shame, blame, guilt cycle I had placed on myself for not speaking up during the test. The shame I had felt about being diagnosed with cancer. The fears I felt at my daughter not having a mother to see her get married because of the cancer.

In this meditation, my inner child stepped forward with arms open wide, seeking an embrace, and said to me, 'I forgive you, my future lives in your heart. Come back to it now.'

The second we embraced, I experienced something phenomenal in that I felt the incredible pain and weight of the negativity. As I breathed in the love from the child, I felt nothing but unconditional love. With every outward breath, I released the emotion.

Once these feelings were acknowledged, I could then reframe the biopsy incident as an experience. This was a turning point in reinvigorating my emotional strength. At that point, I could then accept the diagnosis fully as an experience to be embraced (not fought) and proceed with surgery. Not once have I used 'war language' to progress through my breast cancer experience. I don't fight, for to do so (for me anyway) would mean fighting myself and that little girl inside me.

By embracing my inner child when she was most vulnerable and raw, I could confront the biopsy nightmares instead of being paralysed with fear. The ability to reframe this way enabled me to return to sleep rather than pacing the house like a caged mountain lion.

Brené Brown outlines in her book that shame is the fear of being unlovable. Please sit with that for a moment and take stock of your inner dialogue. Ask yourself right now whether you've talked smack to yourself today 'you're such an idiot', 'you're useless', 'stupid'. These days I literally struggle to write this because I've been decluttering the smack talk for years. It's literally no longer in my vocabulary.

Reframe is one of the most powerful tools you will ever come to use.

 **Mountain lion tamer tip to love your inner child**

1. Be kind to yourself.

2. Actively seek joy in your life.

3. Connect with your inner child.

Depending on the severity of your trauma response, you may benefit from taking these first few steps with a qualified professional. This way you have someone guiding you through a connect and release process and hopefully they don't leave you hanging. There's nothing worse than being foetal on the floor for weeks on end, feeling stuck and not able to process the feelings because they are too intense and uncomfortable.

Wrap-up

We've explored that love should be more than simply a sentiment or statement. It's a feeling you should connect to daily to fill up your happiness bucket. I've explored that your inner child is the gatekeeper to a plethora of knowledge and is often the root cause of why you hold a trauma response now.

Try on the activities listed in this chapter. If you're new to addressing your trauma response, seek support to kickstart your healing journey taking positive steps instead of feeling like you've stepped backwards. Gift yourself the opportunity to reflect on your situation with a fresh set of eyes instead of the existing trauma response. Put the pain aside for a moment and just be gentle with yourself – you're so worthy of kindness right now.

In the next chapter, I'm going to introduce how to pull together all the tools presented so far so that you can feel empowered enough to embrace your life.

 ## Mountain lion tamer affirmations to love self once again

Create a worthy self

1. I am willing to distance myself from the parts of my life that I no longer fit.

2. I attempt to communicate with others as clearly as possible to avoid misunderstandings, sadness or drama.

3. True healing occurs when I gift myself permission to own the arising feelings and then release them back to the universe.

True forgiveness

4. The courage to be vulnerable is not about winning or losing, it's the courage to show up when you can't predict or control the outcome – Brené Brown.

5. I am willing to learn to consciously see what I need to release.

6. I am willing to revisit my trigger behaviours with a view of identifying the baggage I've been carrying.

Surrender isn't failure

7. Trauma creates change you don't choose. Healing is about creating change you do – Michele Rosenthall.

8. Surrender and accept that whatever is happening in this moment, the universe is working on your behalf – Martin Kipp.

9. Sometimes it's not the times you decide to fight, but the times you decide to surrender that make all the difference – Sissy Gavrilaki.

Love the inner child

10. I am willing to learn to accept myself.

11. I am willing to learn how to embrace / explore my self-worth.

12. I am willing to learn to explore my inner child.

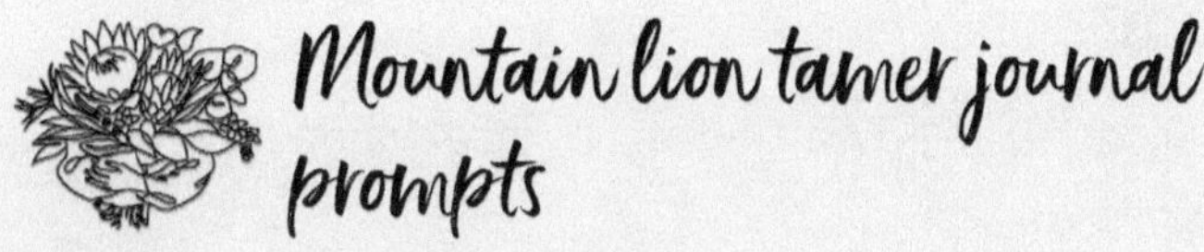 # Mountain lion tamer journal prompts

Create a worthy self

1. Have I placed myself in a cage to feel safe?

2. What needs reframing to free myself from that mental cage?

3. What action can I take (even if only to call for help)?

4. When will I take this action?

5. What am I waiting for if that action isn't now?

6. When I am triggered, what am I being called to look at within myself to allow myself to come back to a place of simply be-ing?

7. After exploring what I need to release, how can I now honour how I want to feel?

True forgiveness

8. What could my life look like if I combined courage, connection to my heart and forgiveness?

9. When I forgive myself, what can I learn about myself in relation to previous experiences which may have caused me trauma?

10. What might I need to let go of and forgive from my past, to see someone as if for the first time?

Surrender isn't failure

11. What does my heart want to say when my trauma response is activated?

12. What are some of the ways I could open my heart to myself or others?

13. After I have encountered my mountain lion, what story of love could I use to help my heart to open again?

Love the inner child

14. Instead of wondering what people think about me, if I allowed myself to connect to my inner child, what might they tell me about my trauma response behaviour?

15. What does my inner child require from me as the adult to feel safe?

16. What can I do each day to experience joy for the pure purpose of getting curious about my happiness barometer?

17. What might happen if I could lay down shame – thoughts, feelings, attitude and internal dialogue – today?

    a. What might change?

    b. Where could I begin?

Chapter Nine

Start embracing life

I'M CALLING IN EVERYONE
WHO'S HAD DOUBTS ABOUT BEING
ABLE TO CHANGE THEIR LIFE
AFTER A TRAUMATIC EVENT.

Yep, I'm talking to those of you who feel stuck and unable to change. Perhaps you've tried everything I have suggested already? Guess what? You're still breathing and deep, deep down, as a human being you are worthy of continuing to experience change and love yourself once again. I am living proof that individuals need to grab our second, third and ongoing chances. You deserve to give healing and happiness another shot.

Stop waiting for a quick fix – it doesn't exist. They are merely a fraudulent ploy by schemers and charlatans who sell magic pills, retreats and all the other hoopla we fall for. You've lost touch with your own medicine – self-love.

Never give up and always keep trying. In my opinion you only perceive failure when you're not focused on the bigger picture. Chase joy instead. You have nothing to prove to anyone but yourself that you are deserving of joy. Healing enables you to learn to like and eventually love yourself once again. Stop waiting for permission from someone else.

It's time to parent yourself. Laugh at life. Love all over yourself. It's time to rein in all the negativity and use the tools to propel your healing steps. It's time to begin by paying attention to your dharma, your purpose in life. We'll talk about dharma in a bit.

Release the need for external validation. You live your purpose in life by ceasing *comparisonitis*, for you are perfect in your imperfection. You live your life by making the commitment to change by using the tools presented in this book to connect with what feels like your first steps. Sometimes those first steps are simply taking purposeful breaths, going outside in bare feet, or simply being kind to yourself.

Following on from the previous chapter of laying down self-judgement, let's expand several ways you can incorporate kindness into your life.

One click of social media and you're caught up in the web of what others are doing and make the mistake of believing that you can step into the life of another and be happy. The point I'm trying to make is you need to learn to be satisfied with your life right now and make the best of what circumstances you have.

You don't find a happy life; you create it

My wish for you is that you make the choice to heal from whatever event in your life pushed you beyond your capacity to thrive. I hope that you become your own joy seeker even in the quagmire of pain and internal disturbance – for that is the light that you seek.

As a joy seeker, I am living proof that a positive attitude pays off. Unless you have experienced a cancer diagnosis and treatment, you can't imagine the emotional roller-coaster and stress that comes with this experience. It's so easy to get caught up in fear. It is scary from the perspective that you must grieve the expectation of the life you thought you were going to live.

Picture me strutting onto the oncology ward with one of my crazy hats – I dressed as a pirate, Captain America, a fairy, princess with a tiara, cat in the hat, and my favourite – 'the jellyfish head'. Nothing but laughter and silly frivolity. I made chemo my bitch.

I stuck affirmations on the infusion bags with statements like 'This is Karen's magic medicine.' I chanted affirmations as I was being cannulised each visit, 'I willingly accept my magic medicine to align me to a place of health and wellbeing.'

I listened to positive podcasts whilst I coloured. I chatted with staff and fellow sisters. I took part in oncology therapy days. I filled my damned cup. I walked in smiling and left laughing – every single time. Even in those days when there were tears, I still left smiling. Oncology day was 110% unashamedly a selfish day. I reframed this to self-more days! I did everything in my power to ensure the magic medicine worked, got myself home and rested.

I will introduce you to the concept of *dharma* – who am I and what is my path? Instead of getting deep and religious, I'll provide you with some alternative ways of viewing your life experiences, which may just enable you to see them as the gifts they are, rather than just good or bad.

So, who the heck am I?

I liken this question to searching for the holy grail. I liken the answer to having the ultimate elixir of life. If you know who you are, you can capture joy bubbles and can truly appreciate the life you live. You are rich and abundant beyond imagination. It's a bold statement, isn't it?

Allow me to introduce you to the concept of dharma – who are we? What is our path? Hinduism defines dharma as a cosmic law underlying right behaviour and social order. Buddhism defines dharma as the nature of reality regarded as a universal truth. Pairing these definitions with Caroline Myss's statement that 'learning the language of the human energy systems is a means to self-understanding', you can formulate that our dharma is simply the lessons you learn from how and why you respond or react to your experience-based life story.

This alternative view of your life, as a collection of experiences that create your life story, may just enable you to see them as the gifts they are, rather than judging them as good or bad. Often recuperation from a challenging or traumatic event formulates not only a healing journey, but a deep understanding of who you are as a person. I often liken healing our deep wounds to our awakening.

LEARNING WHO YOU ARE AND WHAT YOU ARE TRULY CAPABLE OF IS A GIFT.

The religious reference to dharma might not be for you, however, when you Westernise the concept simply to 'Who am I?' and 'Where am I going in my life?', suddenly the door to a room of everything unknown opens to you. What can be surprising is that on your energetic level, you know who you are, but because of the trauma stress response, you've shut down access to this information. You can so easily feel stuck and then your energetic connection to who you are isn't flowing correctly.

When you feel lost or alone, disconnected with your why (dharma), many liken this to being out of rhythm with yourself. Visit the self-help section of any library or bookshop and you're bound to find published work by any myriad of authors who challenged you with their version of how to find yourself.

I discovered my dharma is to discover love through experience. My soul journey is to embark on the role of showing others how to embrace their own experiences and journey back to love. I'm nearly half a century in age and it's taken me this long to figure that out. Regardless of your religion or belief system, I believe now that you are meant to actively work on your dharma.

Embracing your dharma is not a project that you start and finish like a house renovation. It's your spiritual maturing. It's the sum of your life experiences and how well you learnt your lessons. Instead of bragging that I have all the answers, what I will gift you is the wisdom that I have gathered as I've walked my path so far, hoping it is useful or simply to view life with a new filter.

The answers you seek from the universe to what is your dharma are often extremely subtle. Allow yourself to flow throughout your day and catch any 'word vomit'. Create space to capture 'joy bubbles' and gratitude too. This reinforces the need to detach from everything external to you and focus on just you, who you are and where you're at today. Don't get caught up in what has happened in the past or what might happen in the future. It's all about right now. Unless you can access a wormhole, this is the only time reference when you can take action!

In our fast-paced modern life this is extremely challenging. You can taint your ability to analyse with negativity. When you catch the negativity, you are standing in your power. You own the aspects of your story which require amendment. Remember, your life defines who you are, not a single incident. You get to define the pleasure, as well as the depth of your love investment you wish to experience along the way.

In my experience, understanding my dharma, my purpose, helped me stay very motivated to find joy bubbles every single day. After my seven-hour mastectomy and reconstruction surgery, I faced an eight-week recovery and it took all that time just to stand up straight. At first, I could barely walk to the toilet, and couldn't shower myself. I had a lot of time to sit and think about who I am.

Let me tell you joy seekers, don't watch Netflix for hours on end, day after day. So, I walked. Starting small, like to the front door. I repeated this until I could do it without stopping for a rest. I set another goal, the letterbox. Then a lap of the court I live in. It didn't take long until I could take myself on small walks around the block. What I soon realised, because of the incredibly slow pace, was that I became curious. I was observing things in my peripheral vision that I'd never made time for. I found myself getting up early to watch the sunrise because it made me feel good to see a new day start. Then I started walking at dawn with a friend.

Over time, my connection to my dharma evolved because I became quiet enough to listen to my internal energetic language, my power. The ideas for this book and several programs simply arrived in my creative mind. I journalled out the feelings of everything I was experiencing and allowed myself to continue feeling.

I realise that the more I sit in my feelings, embracing the *shenpa*, the more I can access my energetic wisdom and the safer within myself I feel. The result is a growing confidence in my ability and desire to speak my truth. There is contentment feeling like I can step up to the plate and swing at the ball coming my way and it won't matter if I get struck out or smash the ball out of the stadium; I've shown up. I'm present. I'm grounded. I'm anchored to who I am.

Each morning I watch the sunrise and know I am enough. My dharma is to find love through experience. For me that's all that matters. I can now awaken and watch the sun rise, loving myself.

Healing my trauma response, I have changed the story I run inside my head. Collectively we live in a world comprising falsehoods – pretending to have it all together, proving yourself worthy (just look at social media) or performing to gain approval – you have become disconnected from your essence and truth. You've become great at concealing your trauma response – it's like it's been hiding behind a mask.

Remember the *shenpa?* You naturally want to avoid the discomfort of confronting your truth. It's difficult to discuss openly because it makes you feel vulnerable and unworthy. You can learn how to reveal yourself safely within a circle, such as family or friends. In this space, these people become your sacred tribe whom you trust to hold space for you. In the sacred circle, you become more confident to allow yourself to develop your visibility to the outside world. It's like your trauma response stuffs you into a box, and actively taking part unwraps the walls you've built around yourself.

When you allow yourself to share your vulnerability, you are allowing others to see and embrace your true essence. Your inner energy is reflected outwards to others. This creates a shift. I call this 'shining your light'. Group work, such as a meditation or yoga class, can create a deeper, more engaged circle of experiences for you and others. When you feel more comfortable being yourself, more of your light and essence comes through and shines. Information alone won't help you. Sometimes working alone doesn't feel palatable and this is where the power of working in a circle comes into its own. Your ability to remain accountable relies upon you taking action. There is no magic pill or quick fix. Harnessing the energy of others in a sacred circle is incredible.

Regardless of your individual circumstances, there will always be the opportunity, if you show your belly a little, to discover a reflection that is hidden from you but obvious to another. This is because it's often less threatening to see a flaw, a challenge, or an obstacle in someone else before admitting you're potentially the same. Louise Hay refers to this as 'partner mirror work'.

Be prepared to show up fully, especially when you are in the mess of your trauma response. Being honest with yourself can be as simple as being willing to look at yourself in the mirror and practise your daily affirmation or write out the negativity in your journal. The key is to find what action works best for you, remembering it may vary by circumstance. Your transformation from holding yourself back with excuses to putting on your big girl panties and courageously taking action could be as simple as attempting to reframe 'word vomit'. Don't get overwhelmed by this, gorgeous one.

Stepping out of your comfort zone to reveal yourself reduces resistance held within the body. This is where the aches, pains and discomfort originate. You're literally breaking through the physical defensive walls of the survival switch. I highly recommend gentle exercise instead of flogging yourself at the gym.

As a side note, it's worth noting that there is such a thing as intergenerational trauma. Trauma can be directly passed on via epigenetics because you were an egg inside your mother whilst she was gestated inside your grandmother. This means that previous generations' values, beliefs and behavioural patterns can all influence your trauma tale and ability to heal.

Doesn't that just bend your brain a little?

Therefore, the wounds you carry because of your trauma, as well as what you've inherited, can be felt as soon as you get close to shattering the spell and stepping into your sovereign power. For some, it can be terrifying to contemplate who they really are. It can feel safer to remain stuck than to heal. These people rarely connect with their dharma.

Stepping into your unique healing space can feel scary because it means you must reveal yourself, even if only on an energetic level. It means you must face the shadows of those defensive walls and shed the light on them. Shining light on your survival patterns is a form of notifying yourself that this old pattern no longer serves you, it no longer has a hold on you. Western culture refers to this as the path of awakening.

Learning to become a joy seeker is a concept I've referred to extensively. I utilise Dr Phil's phrase, 'How's that working for you?' to reframe anything negative that arises. It's a nice little reality check when I'm feeling defeated. This single question can unlock the door to a room filled with surrender. My experience is that this question instantly supports me to reframe from negative to positive and look at the situation from a different viewpoint.

When you can honestly look at and ask yourself, 'Do I need to know all the negative things I'm feeling right now, or simply acknowledge how they make me feel?' How is the trauma response stuff serving me? What do I gain from feeling like this? When you acknowledge you want to lay down the negativity, because you've realised there's a blockage, you can reframe in preparation for the next challenge you face.

The gift that conscious awareness brings is equivalent to declawing the mountain lion in your fridge. When you empower yourself to realise that you are ready to let go of whatever has previously frightened you, whatever is in the fridge no longer has any power over you. You can no longer be frightened to the same extent because you've detached.

Stepping out of victim mode, where you blame everyone else for your trauma response, is initially incredibly confrontational and uncomfortable. Using the power of reframe and looking at the fishbowl of life through a different lens is extraordinarily powerful. On a personal level I learnt that my 'why' is to learn what love is at its deepest core through the gift of experience. My professional 'why' is to teach my audience how to navigate these experiences as the gifts that they are, rather than as trauma.

 **Mountain lion taming tips for embracing your dharma**

Here are some ways to explore your dharma:

1. Pay attention to synchronicity.

    a. Universe / Spirit / God (call it what you want) is very good at sending us messages. It's time to pay attention! Start taking notice of what or who shows up in your life. Be mindful that if someone or something continues to show up over and over, it's likely that this is tied to your dharma.

2. Follow your intuition.

    a. Intuition, or your calling. is what you feel deep within, that guides us. It doesn't need to make sense to anyone else but you. It's feeling or all-knowing, rather than a voice inside your head. These wisdom messages are preparation for your personal dharma.

3. Know when you've reached a change point.

    a. Our heart space often guides us when it's time to go, step back, or pause. If you have that feeling for change, there's a reason. Your mind might fight you, but your soul knows best.

4. Be aware that the journey path of life isn't straight.

    a. The path to your personal dharma may in fact feel like a spiral. Just when you think you've gotten there, you spin deeper into some aspect. It helps to surrender to the notion that the journey isn't always forward.

5. Surrender ordinary thinking.

    a. Some might call this making friends with the illogical. It's important to know that your dharma is not coming from a rational place. If you are trying to over-mastermind it, you will probably drive yourself crazy, and your dharma will feel even further away.

6. Have a practice that connects you to a greater source.

    a. Whether it's yoga, meditation, watching the sun rise, painting, or walking (especially in nature), it's important to connect with a source greater than you because that's where the energetic information about your dharma lies for you to step into it.

7. Look at the people you admire.

    a. The people you admire represent the greater aspects of you. Put on your detective hat. Where is there alignment or resonance with these people you respect? This can give you clues to your personal dharma.

8. Be serious and be lighthearted about your change process.

    a. If you take discovering your dharma too seriously, you may not actually be able to see it. It helps to have a light touch.

9. Have courage to walk into the mystery of life.

    a. Commit to discovering your dharma, call in a higher level of trust.

10. Allow breathing space.

    a. Your dharma is not something you can 'catch.' You need to take steps, then leaps, and then let yourself breathe. Patience is an absolute necessity. This is an evolution, not a revolution.

Stop seeking external validation

Every time you compare yourself to others, you take the focus off you. You reinforce the neurobiological behavioural patterns in the brain. Your life is your business. And your responsibility. It's time to be accountable. All the medicine and therapy in the world doesn't fix you. It provides you with internal resources – like suppressing symptoms of pain. Learn to become responsible for your own joy bubbles and make deposits in your own happiness bank account.

Wikipedia defines the word comparison as 'the act of evaluating two or more things by determining the relevant, comparable characteristics of each thing, and then determining which are like each other, which are different, and to what degree'. Here's the thing, we are all beautifully unique and individual. Yet many social norms create scenarios whereby you compare yourself to others.

For example, social media creates the illusion of the lives that your friends and family are experiencing. How many sad photos do you see? Glossy magazines with airbrushed models eating chocolate. Jamie Oliver cookbooks – never do you see a burnt pan or a complete disaster in his kitchen. And just imagine if you could have smell-a-vision? Holy moly, that bloke loves his garlic!

Can you now see that your feelings, thoughts and behaviours are entirely yours? So how is it you think that your experience is any better or worse than someone else's?

Edith Eger talks about the common diagnosis within her practice as hunger – for approval, attention and affection.

SUFFERING IS UNIVERSAL, VICTIMHOOD IS OPTIONAL.

I reflected on my recovery from chemotherapy, like most patients would, and remembered the days that I remained in the shower crying for what felt like hours. Whilst the crying was cathartic, it didn't change how the chemo roughed me up around the edges. The crying didn't stop my feet from burning. It simply reinforced how stuck I felt sometimes.

When I used tools like breathwork and meditation, journalling, and working with a therapist methodically, I found the 'gift' and the lessons that I had yet to accept, learn and embrace.

My 'Aha' that evicted me from my chemo pity party was a particular oncology rehabilitation session whereby the practitioner was getting us to discuss the emotions associated with treatment. Listening to a man who had been having chemo every second week for three years was incredibly humbling. Here I was feeling like I had done three rounds with Mike Tyson in the ring after only seven weeks!

At that moment I realised I couldn't compare my experience of oncology treatment even to another patient – because we are all different. There were no obvious similarities to examine between any of us that day, other than that we all experienced the same feelings. We all had different types of cancer. We were all different ages and different mindsets.

I left that rehab session with the knowing that whilst we all have commonalities (we're all human), we are all uniquely different. Comparison doesn't do anyone justice. It robs you of your energy and focus on self and directs that externally.

What I learnt from this rehabilitation encounter was to replace comparison with kindness. Kindness is like accepting a key that unlocks permission to become your own teacher. The only downside to kindness is when you give too much of yourself to another and you're robbing yourself of that loving energy. Some may doubt that kindness is the key. They may be jaded from their experiences. They may look at the trauma of the world with the negative-Nancy goggles. Does kindness solve the problems of the world? No. Does it heal your trauma? If you allow the gift that kindness brings, which is peace from the trauma response, then yes, over time, kindness is golden.

Comparison and the judgements of others are inevitable. It's human nature. One of the most profound tools I used to reframe and remove my negative-Nancy pants is to decide how I choose to respond in the moment. This turns off the stress-based reactive response. The barrier to stopping comparison is the habit you have of doing it. It comes so easily until you connect with how it makes you feel.

Kindness is free, resentment costs you everything

Kindness is the cheapest gift of all. The Oxford Dictionary defines kindness as 'the quality of being friendly, generous, and considerate'. Positive psychology explains that self-compassion is becoming a measurement tool for resilience and a predictor of wellbeing. In the many books I have read, the common denominator is the definition of self-compassion. It involves treating yourself with care and concern, especially when viewing yourself as inadequate, unworthy, someone who has made mistakes, experienced failure or painful life situations.

Positive psychology defines kindness as three interacting components: self-kindness versus self-judgement, a sense of common humanity versus isolation, and mindfulness versus over-identification. Self-kindness refers to the tendency to be friendly and generous with self. Instead of being critical of self with the shame, blame, guilt cycle, how instead could you care for self? Would you be friendly with yourself? Would this kindness then enable you to understand yourself or the situation differently?

Would this be a better outcome than punishing yourself? What might it take for you to realise you are all imperfectly perfect? It's not until you're feeling stuck and downtrodden from the trauma response that you realise you aren't perfect. This is when kindness can be the best gift of all.

Positive psychology challenges the reader; rather than attacking and berating oneself for personal shortcomings, being kind to self offers warmth and unconditional acceptance. The act of kindness allows you to gently and respectfully acknowledge when you're behaving inappropriately or not for your highest good. I would add that when life becomes stressful, society teaches us to immediately try to control the situation or fix the problem. Gifting yourself through an act of kindness, like offering oneself nurture and comfort, will create an entirely unique response to trauma.

Kindness isn't a 'get-out-of-jail-free' card. It doesn't bypass your need to be responsible and accountable for your actions and behaviour. Being kind to self softens the blow that you so often feel from trauma and life itself.

So often fear runs our lives (refer to earlier chapter and reference to biological response to fear). Fears influence what information you recall from your subconscious, reactive behaviours which influence your thoughts, feelings and attitudes.

Kindness creates a safe space within to connect to the deepest and purest version of self. Being kind to self can support you to step off the shame-blame-guilt merry-go-round, step out of negativity and focus on what you can do today, in this present moment. Kindness enables you to self-soothe so that you feel safe and calm. This enables you to reframe any arising trauma response into a simple acknowledgement that something has triggered you.

Kindness can reassure you as you practise embracing the feelings of *shenpa*. Feelings are designed to come and go, not sit and fester like a pile of dog shit. Kindness subtly reminds you to practise laying down those suitcases of crap that no longer serve you feeling good about yourself.

Kindness can motivate you to seek new ways of doing life and change your stagnant routine. Small things like going for a gentle walk around the block get you off the couch. Instead of beating yourself up about sitting in front of the idiot box for hours on end, you can celebrate that you went outside for fresh air and views. Another perspective is instead of flogging yourself at the gym, break up your routine, stimulate your senses and calm your busy head by immersing yourself in nature.

 **Mountain lion taming tips to embrace kindness**

1. Make time for quiet reflection – time is a beautiful gift.

2. Recognise your positive qualities and how you use them.

3. Before bed each night, identify three good things you achieved on that day.

4. Focus only on what is in your control.

5. Don't put pressure on yourself to complete everything on your to-do list. Have the goal to do just one thing and do it well.

6. Slow down and allow yourself to be fully immersed in things you do.

7. Be prepared to own your mistakes.

8. Explore new ways to relax your mind and body.

9. Ask yourself daily – what do I need to thrive today?

10. Practise forgiveness.

11. Stop worrying about what others think and ask yourself – what am I thinking and feeling?

Wrap-up

Kindness doesn't mean spending money. It's about being friendly to yourself – so, be gentle with your self-talk. Kindness is about being generous – when was the last time you praised yourself for achieving another day?

Do you:

- Congratulate yourself for the minor achievements?

- Tell someone thank you when they do you a wonderful service?

- Smile at strangers?

- Tell those you cherish you appreciate them?

We so easily spread kindness to others but rarely show this gift to ourselves.

Kindness is about being considerate. When was the last time you felt triggered by someone, could lay down the suitcase of crap and allow yourself to see the other person? I mean really see this person for who they are in that moment; they are sending you a gift of what you look and feel like because you've been ignoring the symptoms within yourself.

 *Mountain lion taming affirmations to embrace a new way of life*

So, who the heck am I?

1. The more relaxed, I am the more energy I have.

2. I am learning how to feel at peace with my life.

3. I embrace my uniqueness, talents and gifts.

Stop seeking external validation

4. Comparison is the easiest and fastest way to feel unhappy.

5. The only person you should try to be better than is the person you were yesterday.

6. Sometimes I need to remind myself that I don't have to do what everyone else is doing.

Kindness is free, resentment costs you everything

7. Happiness is the new rich. Inner peace is the new success. Health is the new wealth. Kindness is the new cool – Syed Balkhi.

8. Kindness is a passport that opens doors and fashions friends. It softens hearts and molds relationships that can last lifetimes – Joseph B Wirthlin.

9. Kindness is the language which the deaf can hear and the blind can see – Mark Twain.

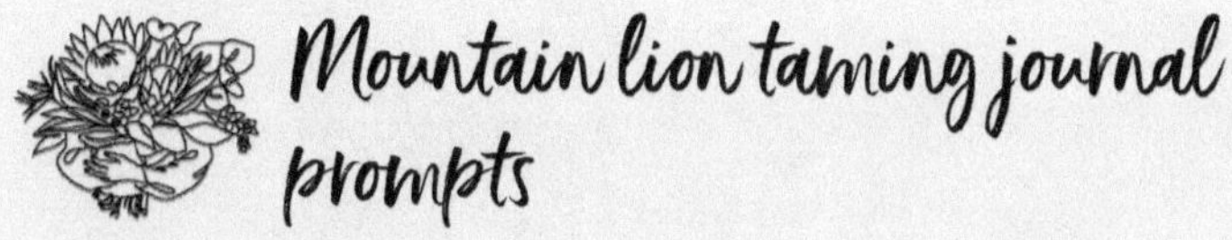

Mountain lion taming journal prompts

So, who the heck am I?

1. What are my unique gifts, talents that I bring into the world?

2. What might I find if I could explore my dharma?

3. How can I show up to myself through self-devotion every day in the right way in the right moment?

4. What might my life be like if that negative voice inside my head didn't exist?

Stop seeking external validation

5. When I compare myself to others, that leaves me feeling...

6. How often have you failed, tried again and succeeded?

7. Instead of looking at someone else's life, what do I want my life to feel like?

8. What are my unique qualities that keep me in my lane?

Kindness is free, resentment costs you everything

9. When I am kind to myself, I feel...

10. Write out five things in your life that you are super grateful for right now.

11. When I'm feeling challenged, the thing that makes me feel good again is...(explain why)

Chapter Ten

Become a mountain lion tamer

WHAT I HAVE LEARNT IS THIS
– AS YOU HEAL WITHIN YOUR
PERSONALISED REALM OF
CONSCIOUSNESS, YOU SEND A WAVE
OF WISDOM THROUGH THE COSMOS,
CREATING A LIGHT THAT ACTS LIKE
A BEACON OF HOPE FOR OTHERS.

Regardless of your trauma experience, you can learn to become a mountain lion tamer by granting yourself permission to live your life to the fullest, celebrate and recognise what it is to have your spirit ignited. Learning to become a mountain lion tamer supports you to connect to your intuition and the energy of your heart, rather than being stuck in your head. Using the tools to heal your trauma tale enables you to speak your truth and allow yourself to be heard, perhaps for the first time.

Call it whatever you want. When you are brave enough to tame the mountain lion in your fridge, this is the point you step into your personal power. It is one of the best gifts you will ever give yourself. When you embrace your *shenpa* or the hook as a gift in your life, you can empower yourself to get out of your own way and create a life that you cannot wait to wake up to. Confronting your own mountain lion is the beginning of anything you want your life to be.

Ready to try some tools presented here? Ready to pause your trauma tale and take action that you possibly haven't tried before?

Some of the first steps to healing simply include increasing your awareness of when you trigger your trauma response. Decipher what a choice point feels like. Learn to discern when to act. Know what tools work for you. Life goes on and the triggers continue until you heal that aspect and then a new set of circumstances arises, so you can continue learning more about yourself.

I believed redundancy was the worst time of my life. I reflected, rebooted and picked myself up off the floor. When my mother died, that 'foetal position on the floor' sensation returned and yet here I am. Somehow, if we surrender and address the components of the experience, we really can heal ourselves and this seems to strengthen us for the next experience.

My breast cancer chapter included a kaleidoscope spectrum of experiences including excruciating physical pain, the terror of closed spaces, a multitude of strangers touching me and an induced fear of the future and uncertainty. I've shared with many people how having cancer also brought me many gifts, including a daily appreciation of needing self-care like I need air!

It has blessed me with quiet time to reflect on what works in my life. This time to myself allowed me to understand and physically feel what I need in certain moments. It has gifted me the opportunity to learn how to address thoughts when they become chaotic. I have become present in my own life, which is like plugging myself into a supercharged universal power outlet!

I now say 'yes' to me first and only then do I consider to whom and how I say 'yes' to others. I also take pleasure in all the little things that I can do. Recovering from massive surgery reinforced my human fragility and vulnerability. It was a truly humbling experience to feel like I was starting from scratch.

What happens to you in life is neither good nor bad. They are just experiences. This realisation was powerful for me. Your values, your beliefs and your choices drive your perception of an experience. The best thing of all is you can change your mind, your perception and your beliefs. You aren't stagnant unless you choose to be. Just beginning one new action might be the catalyst for a ripple effect of a change in your life. You won't know how successful it can be until you commit to yourself.

I often ask myself, as well as my clients, 'If you could view your life differently, would your perception of the situation, event or stress be different? After looking at your circumstances from a different place, what would you now change if you had a magic wand?' Challenging someone to look at their circumstances from a different place can often be an incredibly empowering stepping stone for change. It's also a lovely way to recognise that your experiences simply become gifts or lessons to be learnt rather than being there to torment you.

In this chapter, I'm pulling together all the resources I've presented and providing examples of how you can use these tools to forge a new routine for healing your own trauma response. These tools aim to show you how to accept the perfect imperfection of your humanness. You're not all dark or all light; rather, you are a collection of experiences. You can choose to see those experiences as lessons, or as burdens. Do you use the choice points along the way? These look like those trigger moments when you feel out of control. Yet they are potential gems to address your trauma response and continue healing. Taking empowered small steps is how you change your trauma tale and learn to roar again.

Raw juice is powerful

The Oxford Dictionary defines trauma as 'a deeply distressing or disturbing experience'. Trauma literally leaves you feeling raw. In the first two sections of the book, I referred to science and energy to explain what happens during our trauma response. The result is you get stuck in your own tale of trauma.

There is also a societal perception that all trauma is bad. The definition itself suggests that healing is not possible. However, if you change how you view life, healing from these experiences can be one of the most powerful gifts you will ever receive. While it can leave you feeling vulnerable, you can also learn more about your capabilities in this space. You can reclaim your life by being brave and overcoming your feelings of anxiety and being overwhelmed – driving you to take small steps to feel safe again, like actions outlined in this book.

Even during a trauma response, you can learn to manage your emotions through connecting with your feelings, identifying your trauma triggers, connecting with controlled breathing techniques and safely expressing your feelings through journalling or talking with a therapist. You can learn to use your own response to trauma to seek your purpose or reason for life, which is so powerful. You can reach out and connect with others. Humans are social creatures. Trauma can make it feel like you're excluded from your tribe and therefore makes it hard for you to reach out for help or talk about the incident.

When people in your tribe are aware of your struggles, it will surprise you how much they'll want to show they love you by doing small things for you. These small actions are gifts and how people can show their love for you. There is an African proverb that says, 'It takes a whole village to raise a child.' The support of your tribe can assist you in taming that raw response to the mountain lion in your fridge.

I want to ram home that while 'shit happens' to all of us, ultimately you are in control of how you choose to respond. Without the experience of trauma, Holocaust survivor Edith Eger wouldn't be a world-renowned psychologist and author. Spirituality leader and globally acclaimed author Louise Hay overcame a childhood of sexual abuse and poverty and learnt to correlate body ailments to emotional stress. Motivational speaker and self-help author Dr Wayne Dyer gained a depth of compassion with the experience of poverty and homelessness. World record holder and author Wim Hof shares his breath and cold therapy technique, which supported him after his wife died by suicide leaving him to raise four children alone. Author and co-founder of NES Health Harry Massey overcame spinal injuries and life-threatening chronic fatigue through learning and sharing the energetic wisdom of Choice Point therapy.

These people reframed their horror stories into their new point of power reference. Call it what you want – power, truth, story, journey or even path

– it is all experience. I have used the inspiration of these authors who stepped into their power to live their desired life. Despite their traumatic experiences, these people reframed their pain to migrate forward in life. We are all capable of this.

Take, for example, the rawness from my diagnosis. I purposefully chose not to fight, but to embrace the gift of the experience of cancer. Why? Because I am so much more than cancer cells in my body. Cancer is just the experience that allowed me the space to embrace the myriad lessons to be learnt. This allowed acceptance of my diagnosis and confidence in my decision regarding treatment. While there were aspects of my diagnosis and treatment that were extremely difficult, those times when I was most vulnerable gave me the most precious gifts of friendship and love and a discovery of my own unshakable strength.

Embracing my cancer experience gave me the opportunity to use reframing from negative to positive. The reframing technique works well when you're grounded. It helps if you are breathing with purpose and connected into your heart space. Practising purposeful breath and remaining grounded sends body language to the mountain lion that you are now in charge.

Peter Smith, a leading spirituality hypnotherapist, founder of the Quantum Consciousness Experience and author of *Quantum consciousness: Expanding your personal universe*, explains that everyone experiences extraordinary things from time to time. Yet you often surrender the importance of the experience because of your prevailing mindset.

Smith reiterates what I often hear in the clinic – 'I just want to be normal.' Yet most people do not know what their normal is. They simply follow the societal expectation that is safe and acceptable in the eyes of others. Smith refers to trauma as 'the dark night of the soul', which can shock a person into an awakened state. What if you could allow yourself to feel your trauma response and utilise your new awareness as the first step to discovering your limitations? Might this new awareness support your drive to notice the conditioning that held the trauma response and now allow you to release it?

Just like a seed uses energy to sprout, so does your trauma response. Imagine how your vital life force could improve, instead of running your defensive switching survival program. I am a living example of Peter Smith's principles and continue to receive compliments for remaining so positive during my cancer chapter. For several reasons, I believe this is because of spirit whispering a warning to me and readily enabling me to accept my diagnosis. I listened to my gut instinct and gifted myself time to process the rising emotions prior to, and after, surgery. This gifted me the opportunity to process the fear of the unknown and the fear of my child losing her mother.

That biopsy incident caused a tremendous amount of swelling and inflammation in my breast tissue. The damage to soft tissue, which ultimately resulted in the loss of my nipple, compromised the reconstruction of my breast. I experienced such an intense sensation of grief when I was told that the necrotic tissue had to be removed. I was inconsolable for several hours.

The necrotic nipple was the last vestige of my breast. Losing it was another reminder of the destructive power that breast cancer brings to your life. My nipple also was a physical connection to how I had nurtured my child as I breastfed her. To lose it meant that I had to face my fear of my child potentially losing her mother to cancer. It was exceptionally confronting.

That nipple also acted like a cap on my emotions after the biopsy and mastectomy. Its removal opened a floodgate of trapped emotions. I allowed myself to express everything that I had held deep inside. After I calmed myself down, instead of playing victim, I used the reframe technique. Instead of asking myself a why question, I asked myself, 'What is this all about?'

Acknowledging the death of my nipple after my mastectomy was a gift in so many ways. It was a key to understanding why I had experienced a lifelong pattern of rejection with my mother.

My birth story was traumatic for my mother and she had suffered shock, followed by postpartum depression. When she attempted breastfeeding, she was only ever able to express blood instead of milk.

On her deathbed, during one of our many conversations, she realised that her failure to make breastmilk represented her inadequacies as a woman. This admission enabled her to acknowledge her perceived failure as a mother, which interfered with her ability to bond with me. The gift for me was that I could connect her inability to feed or pick me up to my rejection patterns that I've battled with throughout my entire life.

I wrote a love letter to the universe the night before the surgery to remove my dead nipple tissue. I expressed my gratitude for the experience of having a nipple and its full spectrum of sensations. This deep awareness and new acceptance enabled me to expand my reality beyond what I had ever believed possible. In those moments I realised I could choose to mother myself. I could be grateful for the experience of a breast and nipple and release the grief at its loss.

Understanding that we are holographic by nature and that we can source our wisdom from anywhere is incredibly empowering. Releasing the need to hang on to the old, crusty dead nipple tissue enabled me to let go of the expectation that my mother loved me in the way I had demanded. I could now fully accept that my mother had loved me in the best way she could. My birth experience had trapped my mother in her trauma response.

We're all simply energy and deeply interconnected on a plane you can't readily see, hear or touch. Rather than having me bumble my way through attempting to explain modern quantum physics, check out books by Dr Joe Dispenza such as *Breaking the habit of being yourself: How to lose your mind and create a new one.*

I used purposeful breath and meditation techniques to identify triggers and areas of stress I've struggled with for over twenty years – and simply let it go. On a simplistic level, within your own existence, you influence your physical form with your mental and emotional energies.

Most people can't fathom another person's pain. They can't understand another person's capacity to overcome adversity because they have no direct reference for themselves. There are a couple of reasons for this. You might feel stuck and distracted by your own stuff. You might lack the desire to observe or detect when someone is distressed, or even get a sense that their energy is not flowing correctly. The vibe of another might trigger you. Our modern culture of avoiding your own discomfort can cause you to evade both your own discomfort and that of others. Many people become terrified of someone else's worst-case scenario happening to them.

People lack the willingness to have faith in themselves. They lack the ability to believe in something they can't see, hear, feel, taste or touch. Avoiding all the feels is like living life in black and white. These are the people that believe they need evidence as proof. Those that require evidence have fears, which bolt their feet to the floor. These people haven't been taught that they can choose their thoughts and their actions. These people also perceive what I'm talking about as almost paranormal or witch-like. It's so far out of the realm of their belief system and what society has taught them to believe that they can't process it.

I often refer to Louise Hay's famous quote about responsibility because it provides such a gentle permission to enable you to sit with your *shenpa*:

> 'We are each responsible for all of our experiences. Every thought we think is creating our future. The point of power is always in the present moment. Everyone suffers from self-hatred and guilt. The bottom line for everyone is "I'm not good enough". It's only a thought and a thought can be changed. We create every so-called illness in our body. Resentments, criticism, and guilt are the most damaging patterns. Releasing resentment will dissolve even cancer. We must release the past and forgive everyone. We must be willing to begin to learn to love ourselves. Self-approval and self-acceptance in the now are the keys to positive change. When we really love ourselves, everything in our life works.'

Louise Hay

For example, the next time you crave chocolate, allow yourself to sit with the craving. Ask yourself, 'What is the craving all about?' Are you bored or feeling overly emotional? If, after five minutes, you still want the chocolate, have a small piece and be sure to enjoy it. Don't deny yourself here; the pausing in the moment allows you to reflect on your thoughts and feelings and assess whether you need the chocolate or why you've reached for it in the first place. This technique is called 'practise the pause'. It creates a pause where you get to explore what the trigger is. Remember, you will encounter discomfort.

Now use the same technique for the next time something emotionally triggers you. Take yourself someplace safe and assess what you are feeling physically and mentally. This is a great opportunity to jump into your journal.

Everyone encounters naysayers as you begin your quest to tame your mountain lion. Let them chastise, let them laugh, let them judge. Let these people remain wallowing in their own fears and anxieties. Allow yourself to observe your life and observe your triggers, because this is how you learn your lessons. You can't learn or do another person's lessons.

Being open to a nudge or three

We all have divine aspects of self. We're all naturally empathic, capable beings who can receive messages from spirit, or God (call it whatever you will), throughout our day. There are messages everywhere. You just have to be open to seeing, feeling or hearing them. This is how you embrace the science of your physics and chemistry.

The Oxford Dictionary defines divinity as 'any supernatural being worshipped as controlling some part of the world'. But when you dig a little deeper, it can mean an aspect of your life or the personification of a force. I liken my divinity to that of embracing the powers of the force and becoming a Jedi master. What if you could harness your own force and redirect yourself out of reaction and back onto your path? It's powerful, right?

Your biochemistry incorporates how you intake, assimilate and eliminate food and nutrition at a cellular level. Physics drives your chemistry to perform the effects of stress hormones on your nervous system and the movement of energy within and around your body. Bioenergetics is the study, detection and correction of energy fields in living systems. It incorporates electricity, the raw energy within and beyond a cell, and in body systems. It also incorporates the mental and emotional aspects of an individual.

But where does the energy come from? It is more than just food. This is where embracing the belief in our divinity links everything you know and see to beyond the tangible. You could call this your innate wisdom. Your divinity allows you to believe that you can control your breathing to calm yourself. Get yourself grounded. Pay attention to and learn how to manage your emotional reaction. Embrace these skills to support yourself in finding a purpose, and this helps you to gain confidence in learning how to tame your mountain lion.

You can choose to change. Your choice point is a clear vision of your purpose today and possibly tomorrow because it feels right on a gut instinct level. It is invigorating and inspiring, and it moves you beyond making goals to becoming an extension of who you truly are through small actions. Your choice point moves you out of a trauma response and into joy seeking mode. It is your safe place. It's your connection to your inner knowing, your purposeful breathing, your groundedness and your calm state.

In this safe space and ultimately the connection to your inner self, you can harness your innate wisdom. Webster's Dictionary defines this as 'your sense of belonging to your life, which is determined at birth'.

Pull this all together now and you arrive at a choice point, which is that fork in the road where you must decide, 'Do I remain in this uncomfortable place of feeling stuck and vulnerable, or do I resolve it once and for all?'

Spirit has shared many gifts with me including the connection to my innate wisdom. Some which I've embraced throughout my lifetime and others which got shut down and had to be dragged from under the carpet. Here's the thing, when you can slow down enough and focus on yourself, you too can access your innate wisdom.

The Cambridge Dictionary defines clairvoyance as 'the ability to perceive information using imagery'. Often, when I'm working, I see colours and where imbalances are held in a client's body. This gift for me is infrequent and something I only experience when I'm awake, alert and very relaxed. I have learnt it's not something I need to access all the time, but when I receive this type of message, it's important. However, when I'm alone meditating, my visions are incredible and very accurate in terms of seeing how things have the potential to unfold. I choose to align to this potential.

Clairaudience is 'the ability to perceive by hearing'. I've become used to the sounds of spirit in my head, like the deep voice that spoke to me of my cancer while I was meditating in the botanical gardens. Claircognisance is 'the ability to perceive by knowing'. This is my strongest superpower, which has strengthened since my cancer chapter and my commitment to self-devotion. I can always pick when my close friends are calling me before the phone rings. If I'm travelling somewhere new, I experience a distinct feeling of comfort if I'm heading in the right direction, or conversely unease if I've taken a wrong turn. Learn to listen to these nudges.

Guess what? You have it too, it's called your gut instinct or innate wisdom. It could be hiding in that place where you avoid all the uncomfortable feelings. It is a definite physical experience for me, which can induce a shiver or make the hairs on the back of my neck stand up.

I also experience claircognisance when I'm in nature, therefore, I attempt to walk in nature every day to charge up my spiritual energy battery. When I conduct group sessions, I advise participants to detach from technology and any other external distractions in their lives. Whenever I am teaching groups, I discuss the science, describe a technique and then guide participants through a working example like a meditation or relaxation tip.

SEE IT. HEAR IT. FEEL IT. TOUCH IT. KNOW IT TO BE YOUR TRUTH.

Gifting individuals the consent to a fresh experience in a safe environment builds trust in themselves as well as me as their coach. Teaching in this way enables a person to gain an understanding of how something works, and then choose to take part. This conscious choice dials down any survival mechanism and enables the participant to activate all their senses to respond to their surroundings rather than react. They get out of their head and into their heart space where they can experience the benefit of the exercise. In a simplistic way, this is activating an awakening of a person's claircognisance. Like anything, it takes practice.

I experience this through nature, which allows me to open a plethora of sensory experiences that can induce childlike wonder and calm the nervous system. This leads me into surrendering ordinary thinking, which is where I pause from the how and what that modern culture wants me to think, feel and behave.

Surrendering ordinary thinking allows you to connect to your own inner knowing and gut response. It opens you up to the possibilities of creating a dream life by using qualities I've described and that you've always dreamed about. Surrendering ordinary thinking is like stepping out of your body, looking back on yourself and seeing the bigger picture. It uses the power of reframe, but it's like you're using steroids.

My favourite way to explain this type of surrender is to imagine yourself walking in nature. Look beyond just seeing green. Look for patterns in the bark on trees. Pay attention to what your senses are drawn to – something to see, hear, smell or touch. Ask yourself 'what is the hidden message?'

You don't need to understand physics or see how your neurobiology works to know that you have a brain. Yet some people require evidence of how the supernatural works. It's a matter of trust. Do you trust yourself and your instincts to instigate change in your life? Do you feel safe enough to follow your gut response and take action or are you frozen? I've often been accused of being a white witch and that's a lovely compliment by the way. Yes, I can reframe nearly everything, but it's just remaining connected to my divinity.

There are some forms of mental illness where the disease causes the person to experience hallucinations in which they hear and see things which aren't real. Unfortunately, schizophrenia is a very sad disease by which patients suffer dreadfully. That's not what I'm talking about here.

To enable a client to quickly assess where they are in relation to healing a perceived block in their path moving forward, I often use Portia Nelson's *An autobiography in five short chapters* in the clinic:

Chapter one: I walk down the street. There's a deep hole in the sidewalk. I fall in. I'm lost. I am helpless. It isn't my fault. It takes forever to find a way out.

Chapter two: I walk down the same street and there's a deep hole in the sidewalk. I pretend I don't see it. I fall in again. I can't believe I'm in the same place, but it isn't my fault. It still takes a long time to get out.

Chapter three: I walk down the same street. There's a deep hole in the sidewalk. I see it there. I still fall in. It's a habit. But now my eyes are open. I know where I am. It is my fault. I get out immediately.

Chapter four: I walk down the same street. There's a deep hole in the sidewalk. I walk around it.

Chapter five: I walk down another street.

Allowing yourself to become conscious of where you are in the process of healing your trauma tale is one of the best ways to learn a lesson and get on with life. This is how you tame the mountain lion, gaining a little awareness bit by bit. Challenge yourself to surrender ordinary thinking the next time your *shenpa* arises. Instead of stewing and asking, 'Why has this happened to me?' allow yourself to sit with the feelings that are arising. Ask yourself, 'What could I learn about myself at this moment? Could there be another perspective here?' Again, sit with what arises.

Tune in to your own channel

Use the tools and know that you can tune in to your own unique vibrational frequency, called your 'vibe'. Connecting to your vibe allows you to pause the trauma response by taking a breath, observing what's happening within you and around you, promoting calm to your nervous systems, turning on your solution-orientated parts of the front of the brain, creating a space for you to respond rather than react, and turning on your own radar.

When you're tuned in to your own unique channel, you can then challenge your boundaries because you trust what you're capable of. You can begin expansion of your previous limitations by trying new things and stepping through boundaries. You can ask for help and not feel embarrassed.

Your physical and mental health aren't separate and any stress within either of these energy systems immediately affects your wellbeing. Your trauma response triggers change within normal routines like eating, sleeping, exercising, and even your sense of belonging. Your connection to who you are drives your ability to heal, what you feel, and how motivated you are to change and evolve. Your willingness to seek support, even if this process starts by reading a book, is all influenced.

Wim Hof discusses the study of hormesis. It's a healthy level of stress to enable you to take on new situations without returning to that place of feeling like a hot mess. I liken hormesis to taking another look inside the fridge, seeing the mountain lion and realising that although the animal is hungry, it's on a chain and can't hurt you. You need to act so that the beast will calm. A simple action like feeding it might just do the trick. Hof's hormesis activities include purposeful breath and a two-minute cold shower each day to reset the sympathetic nervous system dominance in the body. Hof creates a fantastic link between your uncontrolled emotions being tamed using physical breathing techniques.

Angel expert and bestselling author Kyle Gray defines a *light warrior* as 'someone who becomes a light that inspires change, a light that serves, inspires and loves.' Warriors reclaim the space that is rightfully theirs, meaning they don't get pulled down by the drama or the expectation of those around them, and simply let their light shine. Gray writes 'the warrior actively chooses their light rather than being pulled into their own worst nightmare by fear'. Gray makes me laugh with his 'no bullshit' language describing being a light warrior as 'essentially being a light worker only with a black belt in bad-assery'.

Imagine if you could view your mountain lion experience as your animal dreamtime wisdom giver. The experience could be a gift. Kyle's reference to being a light warrior is the same as me telling you to turn off the survival program switch and roar your socks off!

People I work with often say that they perceive healing as difficult, like climbing an insurmountable mountain. This is just one mindset which you can choose to change. You can reset so many ailments by reframing situations with afformations and small actions. This is why I've provided so many 'small' actions throughout this book.

Hof outlines how you can affect change in your sympathetic nervous system – that flight-fight-flee response – in ten days, just using cold showers and breathing techniques. The perception that healing is hard can bring us undone. Yet a little perseverance with this small action can provide enormous change outcomes.

If you've felt stuck in your trauma response for months or years, it can take a little while to unravel these behavioural patterns. Your defensive response has become a habit and it's become interwoven into your web of life, so you must undo it. The gift of using your 'roar' or finding your internal power is that you become more open and willing to look at where you're stuck. Learning to tame the mountain lion means it no longer becomes fearful to look at what makes you uncomfortable.

Use all the actions already presented in the book – meditation, purposeful breathing, grounding – anything you can do to get out of your head and into your heart space where all your innate wisdom lives. Embracing the wisdom within your heart is how you tame your mountain lion survival response.

Here is a journal prompt to help you: 

1. Allow yourself to write the story of what's happening right now, any feelings that arise, any thoughts, so that you can deal with it. Once it's expressed on paper, it's out of your head. This allows you the gift of dropping into your heart and exploring from a safe perspective.

2. Sometimes you need a helping hand to kickstart reconnecting back into your heart and out of your head. I often say to people in the clinic, 'I'd like to reintroduce you to a relaxed person, or a calm person, or out of your head.' They then have that visceral experience of what it feels like to be back in your body, back in that calm, safe place and they are free to explore why there's a mountain lion in their fridge, rather than just being reactive all the time.

Wrap-up

I've presented all the tools that you'll need to tame the mountain lion in your own fridge, but also to see what the mountain lion must teach you. I've been talking about the power of the raw trauma tale and how to reframe situations, which can allow you to find who you really are, rather than the reactive version of yourself.

There are many practical tools like breathing, grounding yourself and being able to trust your innate wisdom – your vibe, your inner witch, your inner 'woo-woo' – whatever it is you'd like to call it.

A high-level barrier that is often shared with me in a professional environment is the unwillingness to heal. I call this the nudge. Do the work, allow yourself to get uncomfortable. Instead of reaching for the pill and making the symptoms go away, allow yourself to sit in the uncomfortable. The more you can do that, the more you become curious about what this is all about. Why is there a mountain lion in my fridge?

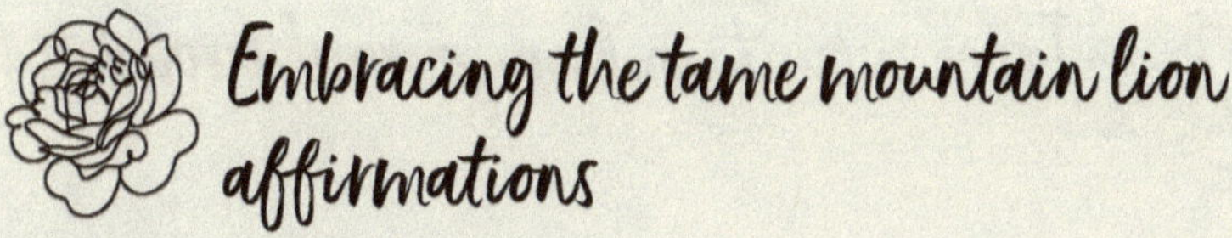# Embracing the tame mountain lion affirmations

Raw juice is powerful

1. I am my own cheerleader.

2. I say yes to me first.

3. I can reclaim my life by being brave.

Be open to a nudge

4. I can choose to change.

5. I surrender ordinary thinking and seek new possibilities.

6. I trust that the universe always has my back; everything is in alignment for my highest good.

Tune in to your own channel

7. I choose to detach from drama.

8. I am open to change.

 # Tame mountain lion journal prompts

Raw juice is powerful

1. When I'm triggered, what is my go-to reaction? Do I fight, flee or freeze? What does this feel like? How long am I stuck in this reaction and what does it take to make me feel safe again?

2. What if I were free to be me? How does it feel like to be free? When I feel, my thoughts include...

3. What enables me to take the first freedom steps?

Be open to a nudge

4. When I listen to the nudges from spirit, I get to experience...

5. If you haven't already connected to these feelings, write about how you would like to feel.

6. When I've previously ignored my inner knowing, what was the consequence?

Tune in to your own channel

7. When I am shining my light as a spiritual warrior, what do I look and feel like?

Author's final note

Writing this book has been a cathartic adventure of sorts in my own life. My wish is it brings an awakening and healing to your own trauma tale. May your horizons be broadened as to what you're really capable of.

The initial publishing of this book is being undertaken at a time of mass societal stress and trauma induced by the COVID pandemic. I hope that my words resonate deeply for you, and the activities can be easily implemented to bring you peace and change the narrative in your world from negative to positive.

To wrap up, here is my biggest challenge to you.

Are you happy with life right now? Or is there something from the past still haunting you? Everyone has button-pushing experiences. The gifts from these events can be far-reaching if you allow them to be.

Use the tools and tips presented here to continue along your own road to healing and walking your own path of change. Always remind yourself that you can choose to change and bloom from within.

Wishing you an abundance of joy bubbles as you rediscover your inner truth and walk your path.

Bibliography

Brennan, Barbara Ann (1987) *Hands of light: A guide to healing through the human energy field*, Random House, United Kingdom.

Brown, Brené (2010) *The gifts of imperfection: Let go of who you think you're supposed to be and embrace who you are: Your guide to a wholehearted life*, Hazelden Publishing, Minnesota, USA.

Brown, Kathy (2012) *Educate your brain: Use mind-body balance to learn faster, work smarter and move more easily through life*, Balance Point Publishing, Phoenix, Arizona.

Chodron, Pema (2009) *Taking the leap: Freeing ourselves from old habits and fears*, Shambhala Publications, Boston, Massachuetts.

Dunn, Cassandra (2019) *Crappy to happy: Simple steps to live your best life*, Hardie Grant Books, Melbourne.

Eger, Edith (2020) *The gift: 12 lessons to save your life*, Penguin Random House, United Kingdom.

Fraser, Peter & Massey, Harry, & Wilcox, Joan Parisi (2008) *Decoding the human-body field: The new science of information as medicine*, Healing Arts Press, Vermont, USA.

Fraser, Peter H (2012) *Energy and information in nature: A collection of papers of the NES Health theory of the human-body field*, Choice Point Communications, Poole, United Kingdom.

Gray, Kyle (2017) *Light warrior: Connecting with the spiritual power of fierce love*, Hay House, United Kingdom.

Hay, Louise (1999) *You can heal your life*, Hay House, New York, USA.

Hof, Wim (2020) *The Wim Hof method: Activate your potential, transcend your limits*, Penguin Random House, Great Britain.

James, Matt, 'Ho'oponopono: How to practice it in 4 simple steps', Source: https://www.laughteronlineuniversity.com/hooponopono-4-simple-steps/

Kirkwood, John (2016) *The way of the five elements: 52 weeks of powerful acupoints for physical, emotional, and spiritual health*, Singing Dragon, an imprint of Jessica Kingsley Publishers, Great Britain.

Krebs, Charles & O'Neill McGowan, Tania (2016) *Energetic kinesiology: Principles & practice*.

Levine, Peter A (1997) *Waking the tiger: Healing trauma*, North Atlantic Books, California.

Mooney, Jacque (2000) *Simply the brain: Introduction to the brain*, Mooney, Melbourne Australia.

Myers, Pam & Worth, Sally (2011) *Rekindled ancient wisdom affirmations: Book 1*, Ancient Perceptions, Rutherford, New South Wales, Australia.

Myers, Pam & Worth, Sally (2011) *Physical body affirmations: Rekindled ancient wisdom affirmations: Book 2*, Ancient Perceptions, Rutherford, New South Wales, Australia.

Myers, Pam & Worth, Sally (2017) *Programme Affirmations: Rekindled ancient wisdom affirmations: Book 3*, Ancient Perceptions, Rutherford, New South Wales, Australia.

Myers, Pam & Worth, Sally (2020) *Emotion affirmations: Rekindled ancient wisdom affirmations: Book 4*, Ancient Perceptions, Rutherford, New South Wales, Australia.

Myers, Pam & Worth, Sally (2020) *Sabotage affirmations: Rekindled ancient wisdom affirmations: Book 5*, Ancient Perceptions, Rutherford, New South Wales, Australia.

Myss, Caroline (1996) *Anatomy of the spirit: The seven stages of power and healing*, Harmony Books, New York, USA.

Phillips, Helen (September 2006) 'Introduction: The human brain', *New Scientist*, https://www.newscientist.com/article/dn9969-introduction-the-human-brain/

Robbins, Anthony (1991) *Awaken the giant within*, Simon & Schuster, Great Britain.

Robbins, Mel (June 2011) 'How to stop screwing yourself over', Source: https://www.ted.com/talks/mel_robbins_how_to_stop_screwing_yourself_over

St John, Noah (2013) *The book of afformations: Discovering the missing piece to abundant health, wealth, love, and happiness*, Hay House.

Schucman, Helen (1976) *A course in miracles*, New York, Viking, The Foundation for Inner Peace, 2007, The Foundation for Inner Peace, 3rd ed.

Smith, Peter (2015) *Quantum consciousness: Expanding your personal universe*, October Grey Media, Warrandyte, Victoria, Australia.

Stone, Dr Randolph (1985) *Health building: The conscious art of living well*, CRS Publications, USA.

Todd, Dr Wayne (2015) *SD protocol: Achieve greater health by learning to balance your physical, chemical and emotional wellbeing.*

Turner, Kelly A (2014) *Radical remission: Surviving cancer against all odds: The nine key factors that can make a real difference*, Harper Collins, New York.

van der Kolk, Bessel (2014) *The body keeps the score: Brain, mind, and body in the healing of trauma*, Penguin Random House, Great Britain.

About the author

Karen Humphries has a mission to support people to rewrite their trauma tale and renew their life by choosing to change, so they can bloom from within.

Karen is a clinical kinesiology practitioner, wellness coach, podcaster and meditation facilitator (to name a few). She's renowned for her laughter and having the superpower to reframe all things negative back into the light. Karen's passion and life purpose is to support those who have been tripped over by life experiences, and show people how to embrace the gifts that life provides.

Karen believes and advocates that we all have stuff. Learning to become willing to explore your experiences and associated stress patterns can readily empower you to arrive at a space where you can shine your light brightly to the world.

Karen is a wife, mother of a teenage daughter and slave to two chocolate labs. Together they live in regional Victoria. She understands the constant juggle to achieve a balance between being a busy mum, self-love and success.

Karen appreciates the joy of good health. She loves sharing her high vibe passion for life and laughter with those motivated for change!

Karen understands people and their stress behaviours, triggers and patterns. She creates inviting environments which support individual clinical work and group participation, as well as encouraging team building and collaboration.

Karen's corporate services extend to:

- Facilitated 'resilience' training, including informal 'team building' programs

- Empowerment and motivational cancer ambassador workshops, programs and campaigns

- Conference presentations and workshops1:1 individual and corporate 'facilitated change' sessions

- Online **Above & Beyond Group** support program

- **Sacred Circle Intuitive Meditation** Group program (8 module course)

- Online Training Programs.

Want more of Karen?

Website: www.karenhumphries.net.au

Instagram: www.instagram.com/karenhumphries_changechick/

Facebook: www.facebook.com/changechick/

LinkedIn: www.linkedin.com/changechick/

Acknowledgements

To say I'm proud of this book would be an understatement. If I'm to be honest, this started as my own therapeutic recovery from PTSD. The passion to support other people to learn to 'roar' took over as a calling, and has been completed during the 'in-between' moments of life. I've had the dream to publish a book for over two decades, but it wasn't until I was diagnosed with breast cancer and had 'some time' up my sleeve that I actually sat and wrote. For those who know me well, sitting isn't really my thing.

This has definitely been a group effort, and I've been blessed with the best to achieve the finished product.

Firstly, let me thank my friend Caitlin Grace for her encouragement right at the start and then throughout the entire writing journey.

Thanks to Leah Mether for writing her own book *Soft is the new hard* and referring me to the incredible book writing coach Kath Walters. Kath held my hand figuratively. Thanks to the pandemic we still haven't met in person, but boy oh boy have we connected over the many zoom and telephone calls. Kath's talent is to capture your idea and take you through her process that draws out all the good stuff. Kath, I am so grateful for your compassionate and kind feedback to this novice writer.

There are many stories from my many years of clinical experience, from a broad range of people who have allowed me to show them how to tame their trauma tale. Thank you for your trust and willingness to change. Whilst their names are changed to protect their privacy, their real stories are still meaningful and true. I hope I've captured them in a way that may be familiar to you, so that you can easily understand the message I'm attempting to convey.

To my first readers, Jacque Mooney (Simply the Brain), Erin Miller (Erin Miller – Intuitive Guide and Mentor), Natasha Berta (Connected Marketing), Claire Wakefield (Natural Body Lab) and Caitlin Grace – thank you for your faith in me, time investment, generous feedback and loving direction. We are so much more than professional colleagues, and I'm proud to call you my soul sister.

I'll be honest and admit I was terrified to send my first readers the first rough draft for fear of judgement or embarrassing myself. Your feedback throughout the book brought me literally to tears – that I had nailed the soul science, the message, and that my roar is a story worth sharing. Still crying tears of happiness and still saying thank you from the bottom of my heart.

A huge shout out to Sylvie Blair at BookPOD – right from our first discovery call you got me. You understood that I write like Jeff Fenech (ex Olympic boxer) talks and still were able to fix all my grammatical errors. Thank you for aligning me to the perfect editor Sarah Lindenmayer whose kind and considerate words made me believe that I could pull this off.

And last but by no means least, my change tribe. For my late mother, Helen, for raising me to be strong, educated and independent. She always quietly encouraged me to follow my heart (and gut) in all things. Thank you for showing me the way forward as a 'joy seeker'.

To my husband Andrew for quietly waiting with open arms as I navigated the cancer chapter and then PTSD. May we roar together another twenty years!

To my brother Mark, for leading the way down the publishing path.

To the goddess gang, Robi, Jen and Mettie, for the hugs, laughter, shared tears and unconditional love. Our collective light shines bright regardless of whether we are together or apart.

To Tanya, for always saying 'yes I can'. You are the sensible and stable one of us, and I promise to remain your feral friend until the end.

To the army of boozy sisters who cooked me meals, drove me around town, had cuppa catch-ups with me, and gave hugs, well wishes and love during my cancer treatment and seven surgeries –regardless of how busy you are, you always rose with your hand up anytime I asked. I'm eternally grateful.

To Matt and Gabrielle, your unconditional loving support has been tremendous for both myself, Andrew and Lulani. Your never-ending encouragement meant I could capture my roar on every page. May we continue to travel, explore and fill our hearts with love and bellies with cake!

As you can see, it's taken a tribe to get this project completed. But that's the experience of life, isn't it? Remember that next time you find a mountain lion in your fridge.

www.ingramcontent.com/pod-product-compliance
Lightning Source LLC
Chambersburg PA
CBHW021242060726

47590CB00005B/1868